NEWDRAWING
NEWJERSEY

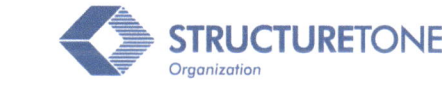

Drawing Together Public Projects Sponsor

VICTORY HALL PRESS

VICTORY HALL DRAWING ROOMS 180 GRAND ST JERSEY CITY NJ

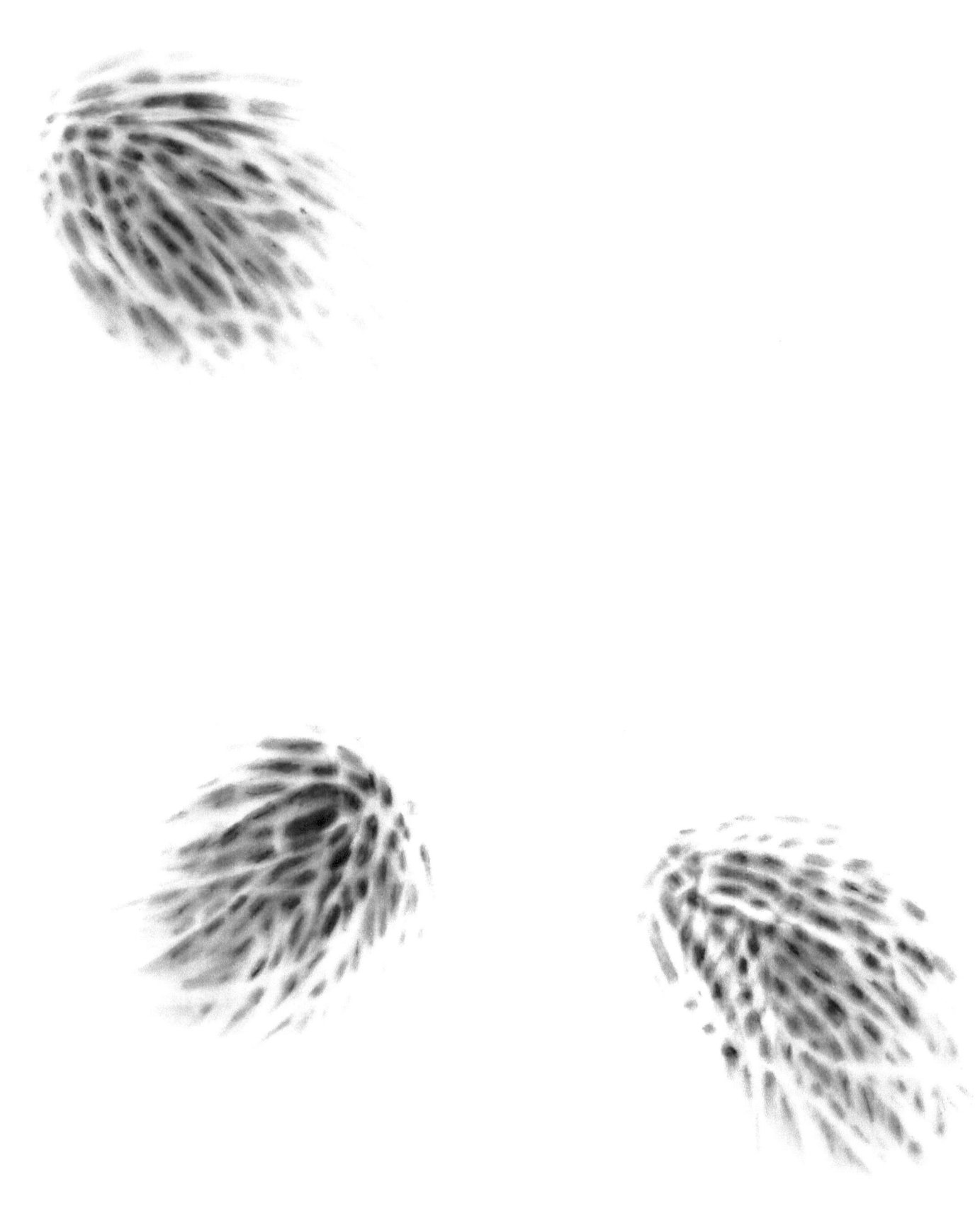

Anne Novado; Three Wee Ones Six; 2011; Graphite on vellum 17.75" x 16.5"

TABLE OF CONTENTS

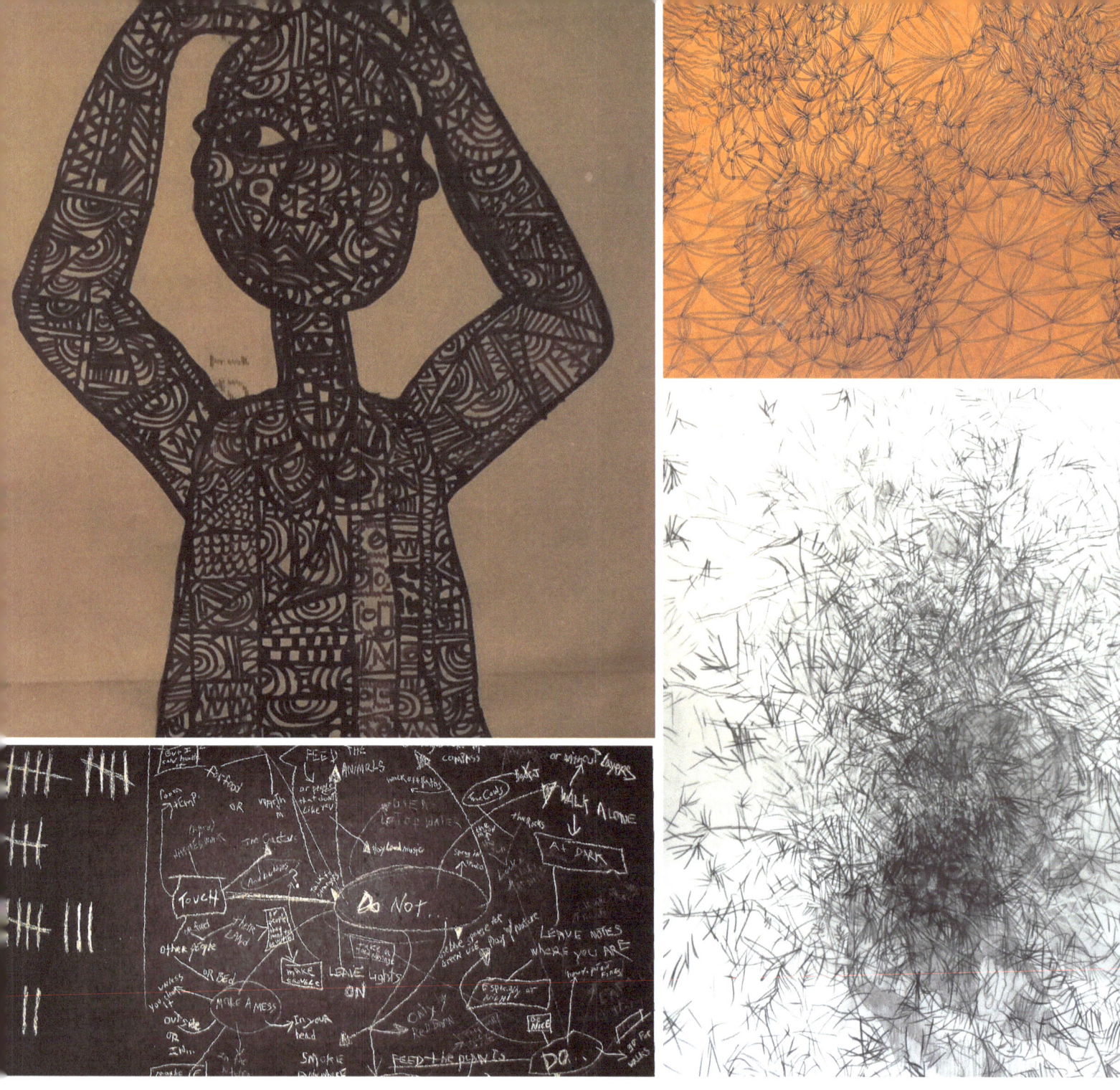

DRAWINGROOMS

New Drawing New Jersey, 06/03/16 - 07/03/16

New Drawing New Jersey brings together some of the best artists currently working in drawing from across the state to Jersey City's Drawing Rooms. Anne Trauben, Drawing Rooms' Curator, asked curators throughout New Jersey to join with her in choosing artists for this exhibition by recommending artists who have shown consistent excellence and innovation in drawing. Anne connected with these artists, working with them to choose exciting, masterful, and diverse viewpoints in drawing. The exhibition spans nine gallery rooms. Each artist is represented by a select body of work with one artist per room.

Curators who nominated artists for this year's exhibition include Donna Gustafson PhD., Curator, Rutgers' Zimmerli Gallery, New Brunswick; Jeanne Brasile, Gallery Director, Seton Hall's Walsh Gallery, Newark; Mary Birmingham, Curator, Visual Arts Center of New Jersey, Summit; Midori Yoshimoto, Gallery Director and Curator at NJCU, Jersey City; Anonda Bell, Director and Chief Curator, Rutgers' Paul Robeson Gallery, Newark, and Victor Davson, Director, Aljira, Newark.

Drawing Rooms is very excited to present our first statewide survey of drawing. An understanding of drawing as vital to development and innovation in the visual arts is at the heart of all we do. In our three years of exhibition programming, we have featured drawing, often exploring its creative relationships to painting, and have found the principles and processes of drawing in three dimensional forms as well. As an art-space on the edge of the Jersey side of the Hudson, we have worked towards fulfilling our potential in making a place of community for New Jersey and New York artists to know each other and exhibit and work together. In presenting these NJ artists here working purely in drawing, we recognize and are proud of their accomplishments and hope to connect them to a wider audience.

Artist's themes in the exhibit explore drawing as both a conceptual and expressive process. Pat Brentano's realistic, environmental renderings suggest she is one with nature. Ibou Ndoye's monumental figures draw from both his African and American culture. Harriet Finck builds graphic linear marks into shimmering, iridescent patterns. Joseph Gerard Sabatino produced a chart-like, arcane writing system during a period of self-imposed isolation. Caroline Burton's expansive grid drawings describe a three-dimensional movement in space. Biomorphic, animated beings seem to take shape and emerge from Anne Novado' swirls of graphite. Marsha Goldberg's delicate smoke forms document political upheaval in the Middle East. In the energetic, chaotic works by Alaine Becker, drawn line and black and white masses seem like living beings pushing against their environment. Heejung Kim's web of transcendent pattern and radiant human shapes illumine an invisible world.

One of the best aspects of this project is how it gave us an opportunity to interact with arts professionals from across the state, many of whom have been working for years developing their institutions and exhibitions, promoting New Jersey artists. We are grateful to the curators, art centers and museums throughout New Jersey that worked with us on this project and thank them all for their ongoing support, involvement and trust in us as we continue to establish Drawing Rooms as a vital space for contemporary art in Hudson County.

James Pustorino
Executive Director

Anne Trauben Curator
Assistant Director

ALAINE BECKER

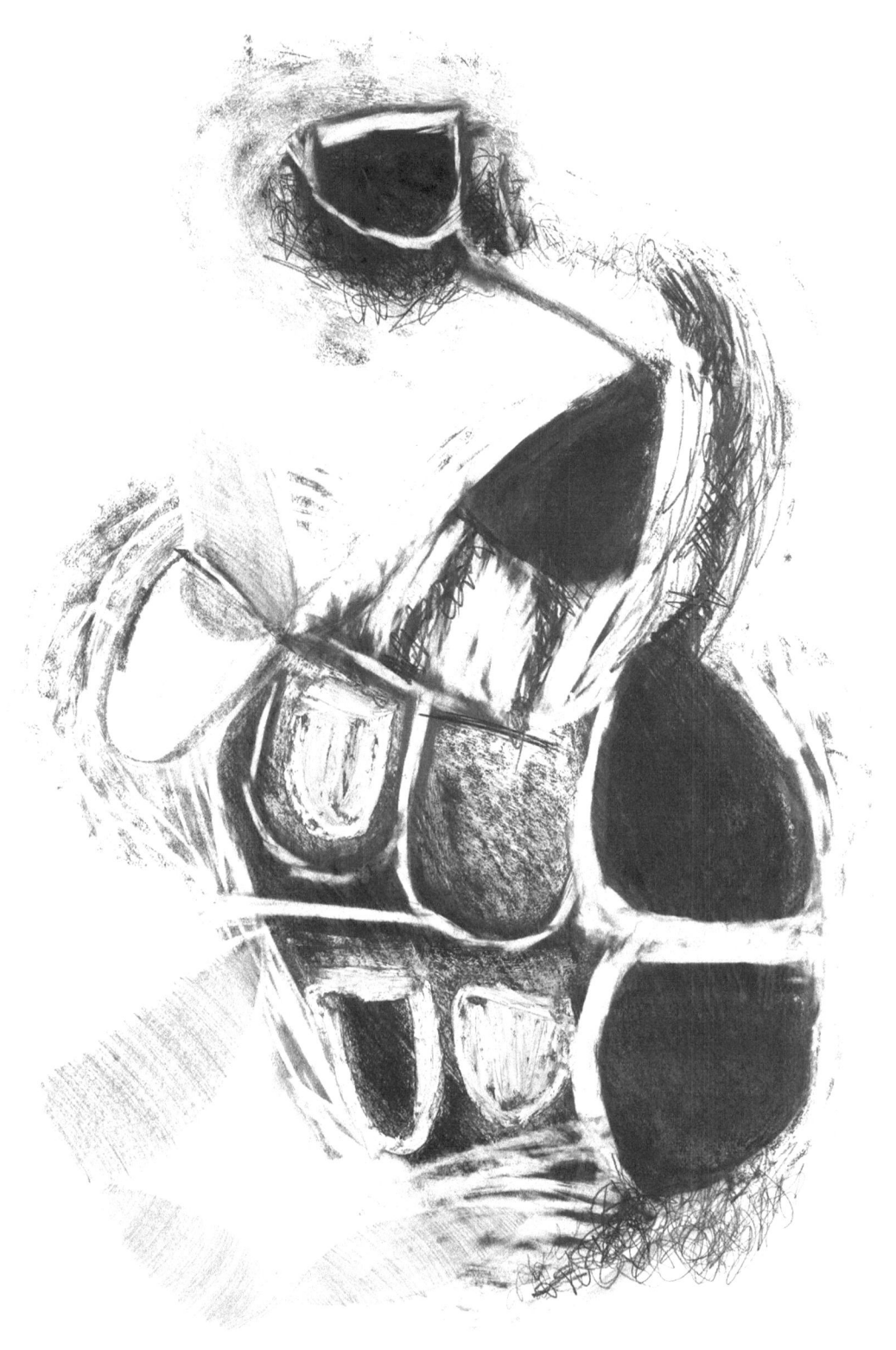

Fools Cap; 2016; Graphite, pastel, oil pastel, conte, on hot press paper; 30" x 22"

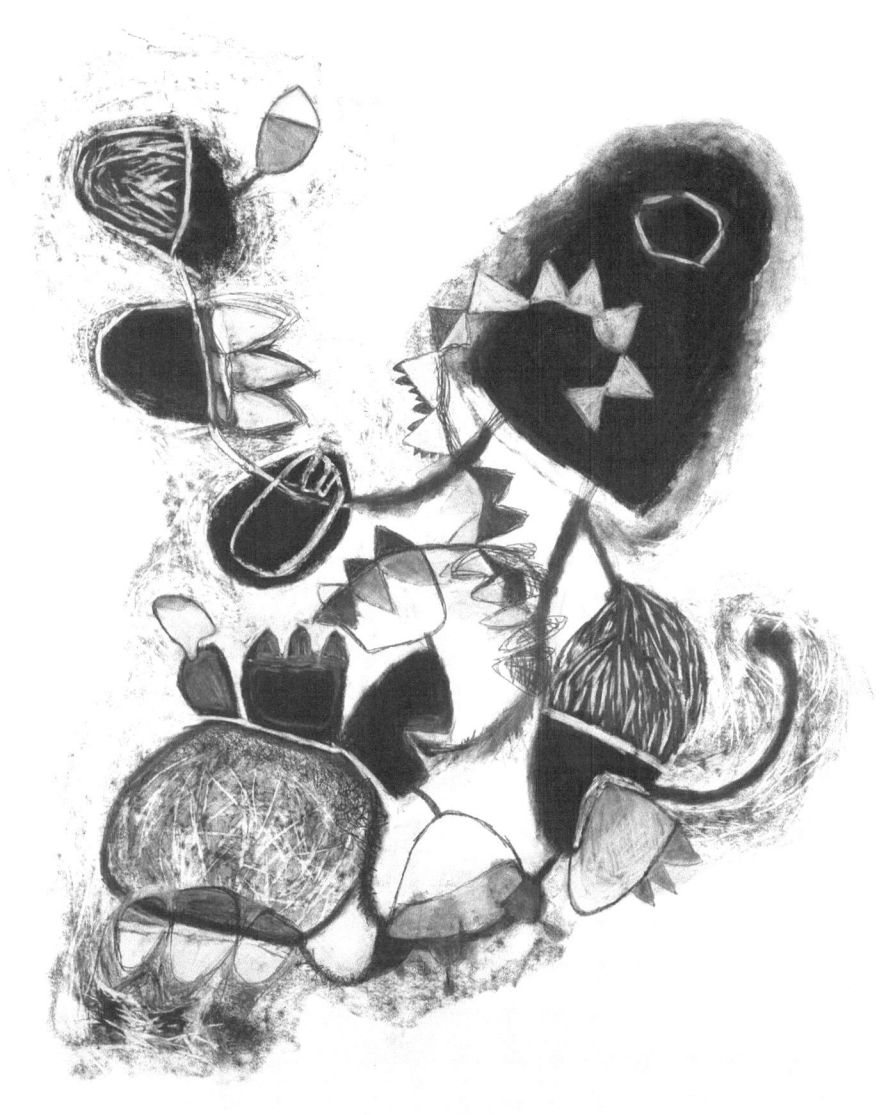

Odin; 2016; Graphite, pastel, oil pastel, conte, on hot press paper; 60" x 51"

ABOUT

Alaine Becker is a NJ artist working on paper. She holds a BFA from the State University of New York College at Purchase. Ms. Becker has exhibited her work throughout the state of NJ. She received a Fellowship from The New Jersey State Council on the Arts, the Geraldine R. Dodge Foundation and an award for a residency to The Virginia Center for the Creative Arts.

"I'm searching for a new visual language and techniques using the basic materials of drawing. There is no agenda here other than the freedom to explore drawing abstractly." - A.B.

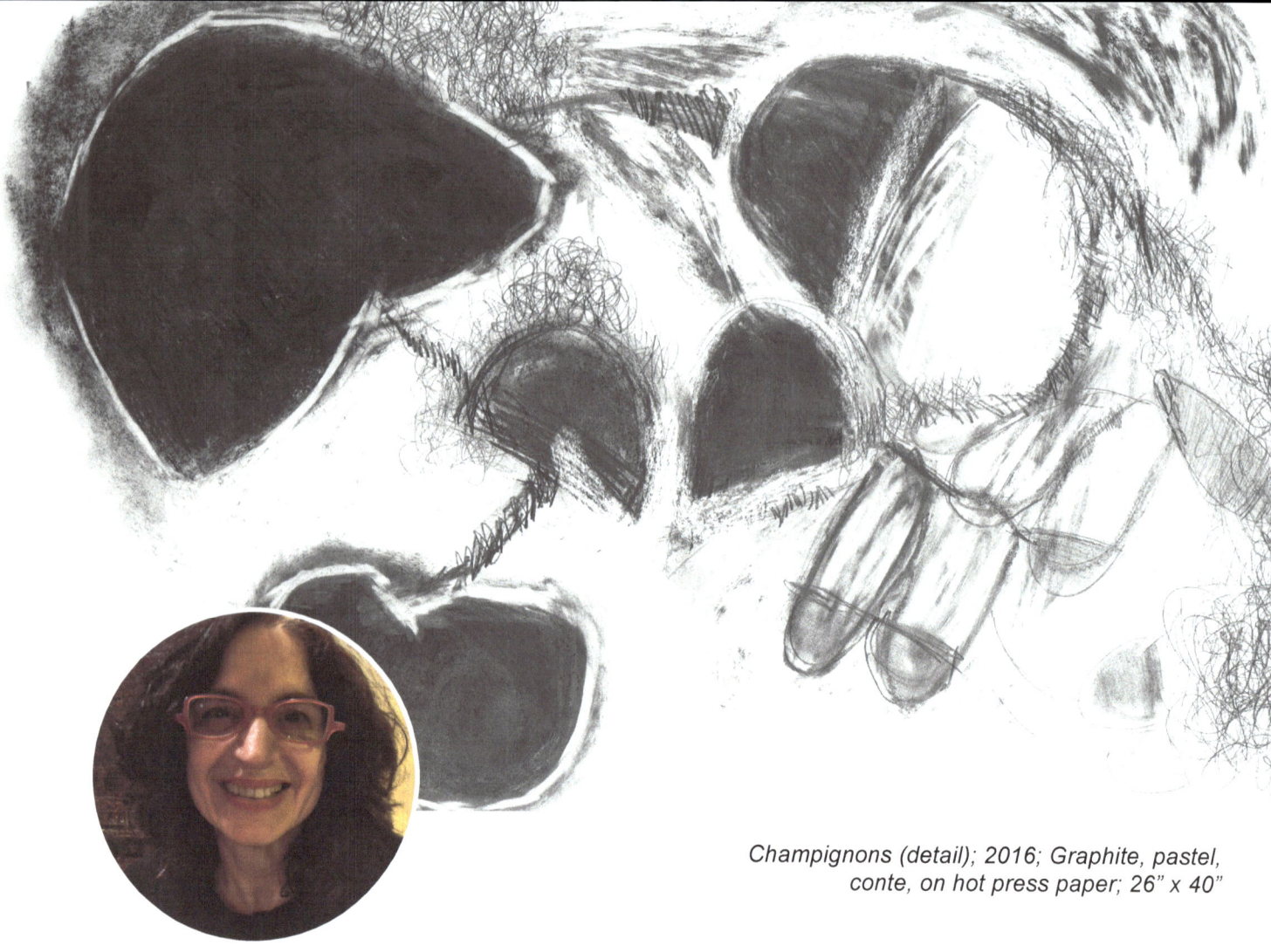

Champignons (detail); 2016; Graphite, pastel, conte, on hot press paper; 26" x 40"

DRAWING ROOMS INTERVIEW

DR: Please tell me about your work.
AB: These are drawings about exploring, finding what I can do with my materials and how I can expand a visual language.

DR: What got you interested in drawing?
AB: Drawing is what I have always done. There was never a time when I was not drawing.

DR: What is your intention in making these drawings?
AB: To see how far I can push these drawings.

DR: Where does your exploration with drawing take you?
AB: This series is the first time I am working without a subject. I am still seeing where it will take me. I find it very exciting.

DR: How is what you are drawing unique?
AB: These drawings have a richness in the texture that I find exciting.

DR: Do you set up constraints or rules to follow? If so, do you stick to your rules or break them? Why or why not?
AB: I have limited myself to graphite, white pastel, white oil pastel, and white and grey conte. The forms must be connected, there are no "floating" forms.

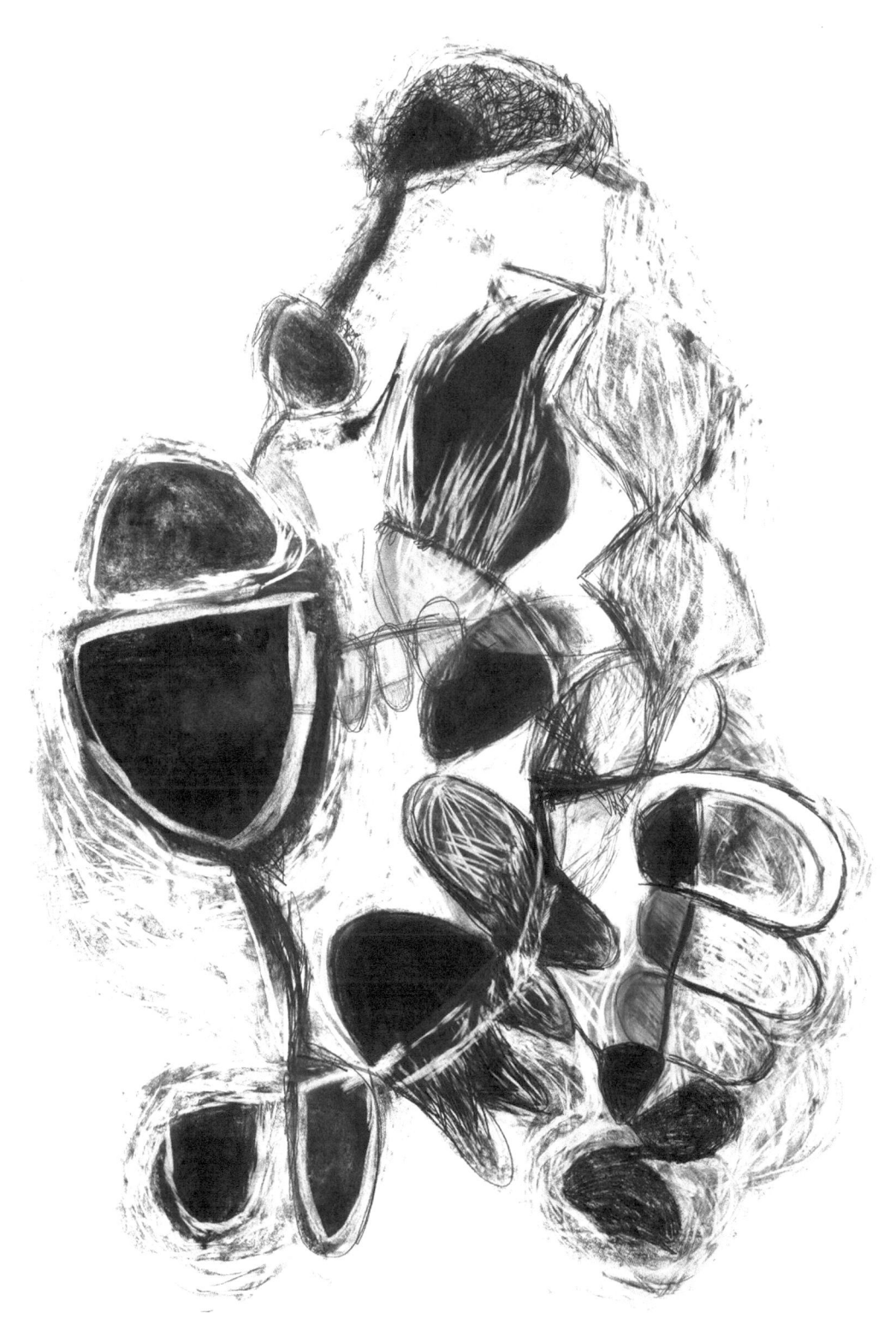

Hoarder; 2016; Graphite, pastel, oil pastel, conte, on hot press paper; 72" x 51"

ANNE NOVADO

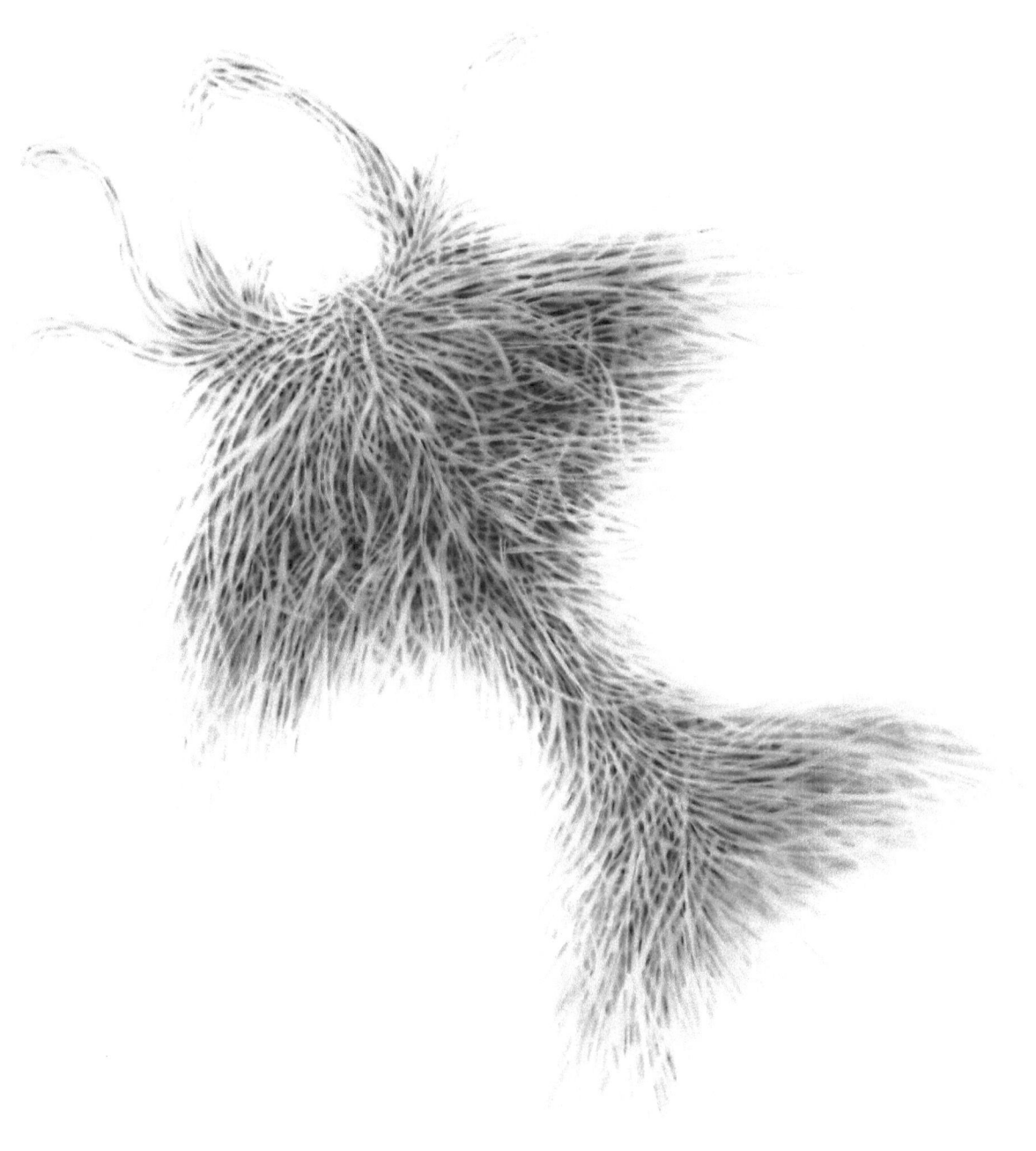

Biomorphic Form Floating on an Angle; 2009; Graphite on vellum; 30.5" x 28.5"x 1"

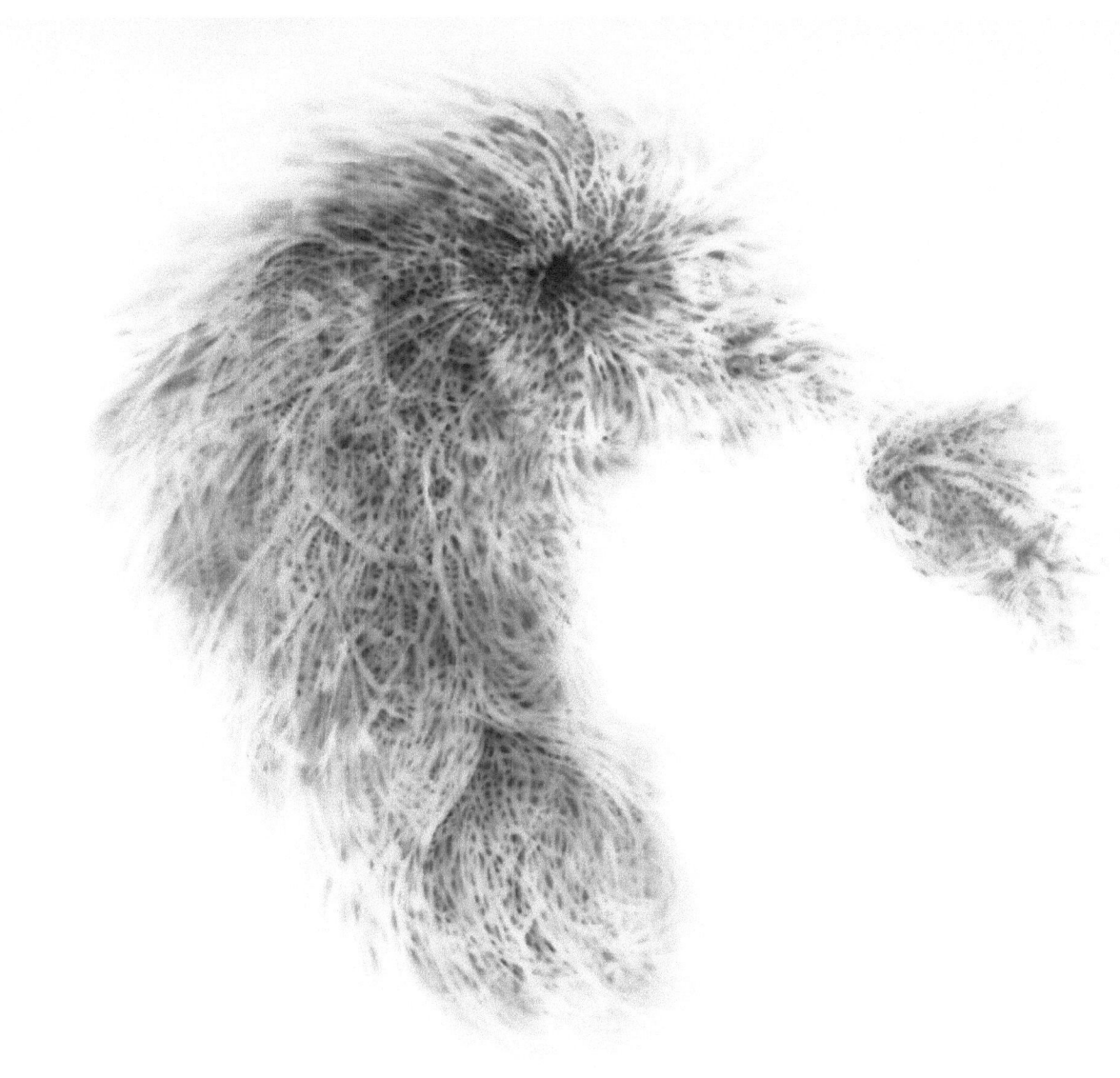

Biomorphic Form with Appendage; 2006; Graphite on vellum; 33" x 36" x 1"

ABOUT

Formerly a resident of Syracuse, NY, Anne Novado relocated to Jersey City in early 2016. Her work has been exhibited in California, NY, NJ, New England, and Iceland. She has taught drawing at Syracuse University and Onondaga Community College. Anne holds a BFA and MFA from Syracuse University. Anne will be openning Novado Gallery in Jersey City in the summer of 2016.

"These drawings occupy an odd and curious place between the familiar and the bizarre, where the viewer often tries to identify something in them that is recognizable, but as these are abstract forms, the familiar association stops short." - A.N.

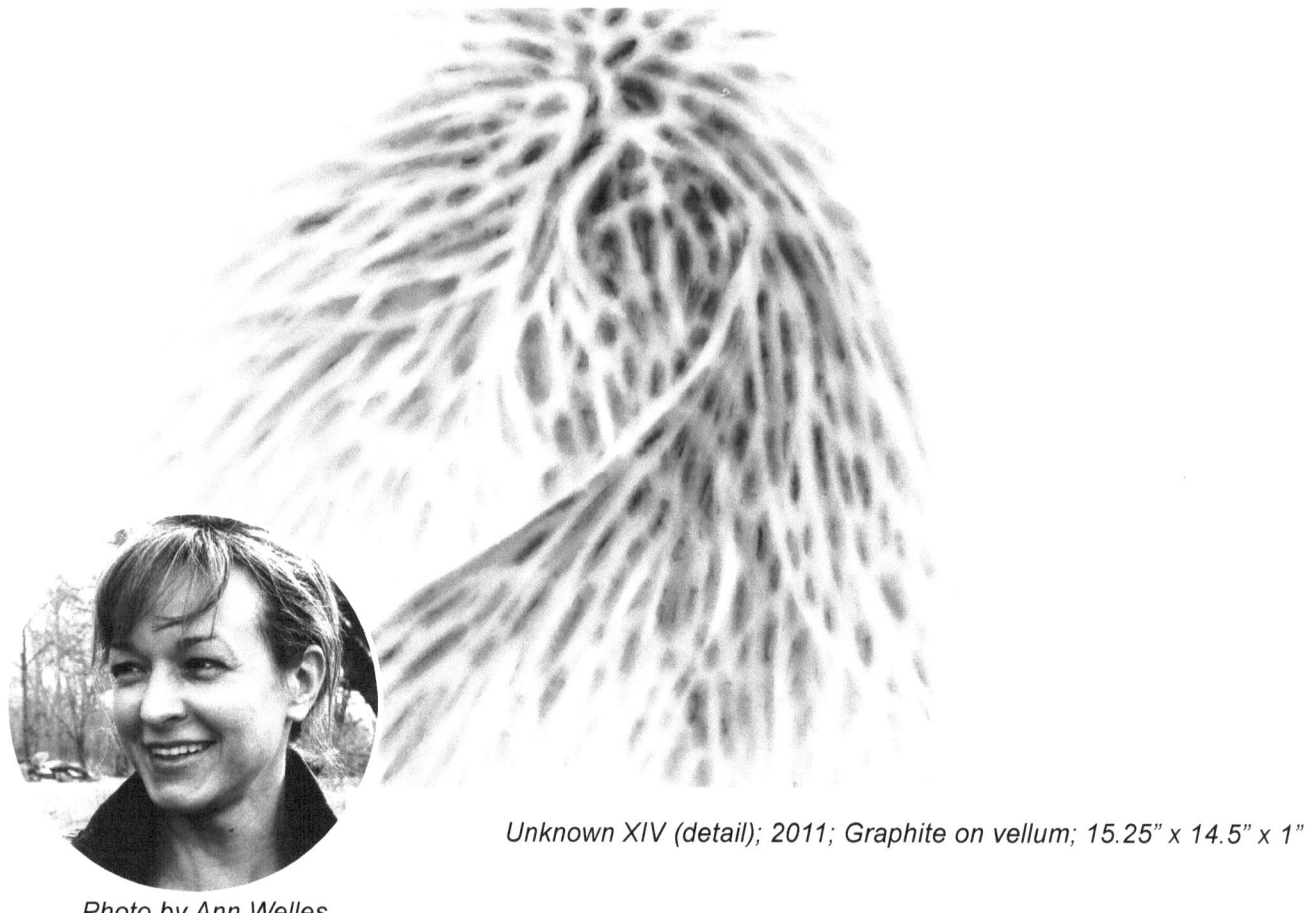

Unknown XIV (detail); 2011; Graphite on vellum; 15.25" x 14.5" x 1"

Photo by Ann Welles

DRAWING ROOMS INTERVIEW

DR: Please tell me about your work.
AN: My earlier biomorphic drawings arose from my interest and observation of natural phenomena, environmental blunder, mutation, hybridity and organism/animal behavior. The more recent drawings came about after I left a long marriage and sheltered life. I drove cross country solo a few times for a former employer, and met and observed interactions of people from all walks of life, which I think it has filtered into the work.

DR: What got you interested in drawing?
AN: I have been drawing longer than I can remember. In my adult life, I appreciate the immediacy of the creative drawing process.

DR: What is your intention in making these drawings?
AN: To lose myself in the process of drawing "things" that only exist as drawings. Maybe I'll make a few that are successful, and have fun while doing it.

DR: Where does your exploration with drawing take you?
AN: On an adventure of the unknown. Time evaporates as well.

DR: How is what you are drawing unique?
AN: These drawings are non-derivative.

DR: Do you set up constraints or rules to follow? If so, do you stick to your rules or break them? Why or why not?
AN: I was initially interested in abstract drawing. However, the images have become more character based. Someone referred to them as being "Seussian". These things are best left undirected.

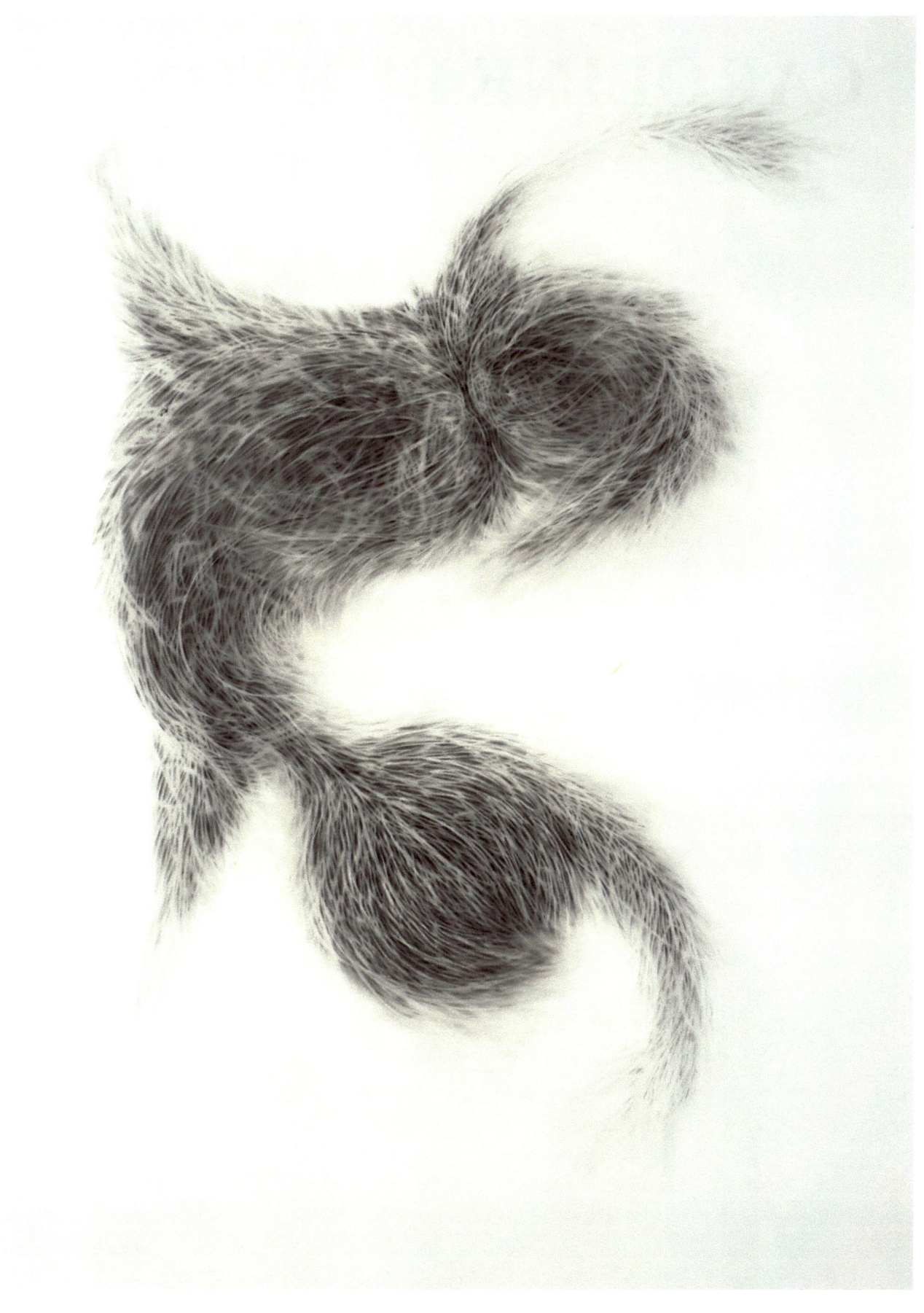

Large Unknown Biomorphic Form; 2011; Graphite on vellum; 49.5 x 42" x 2"

CAROLINE BURTON

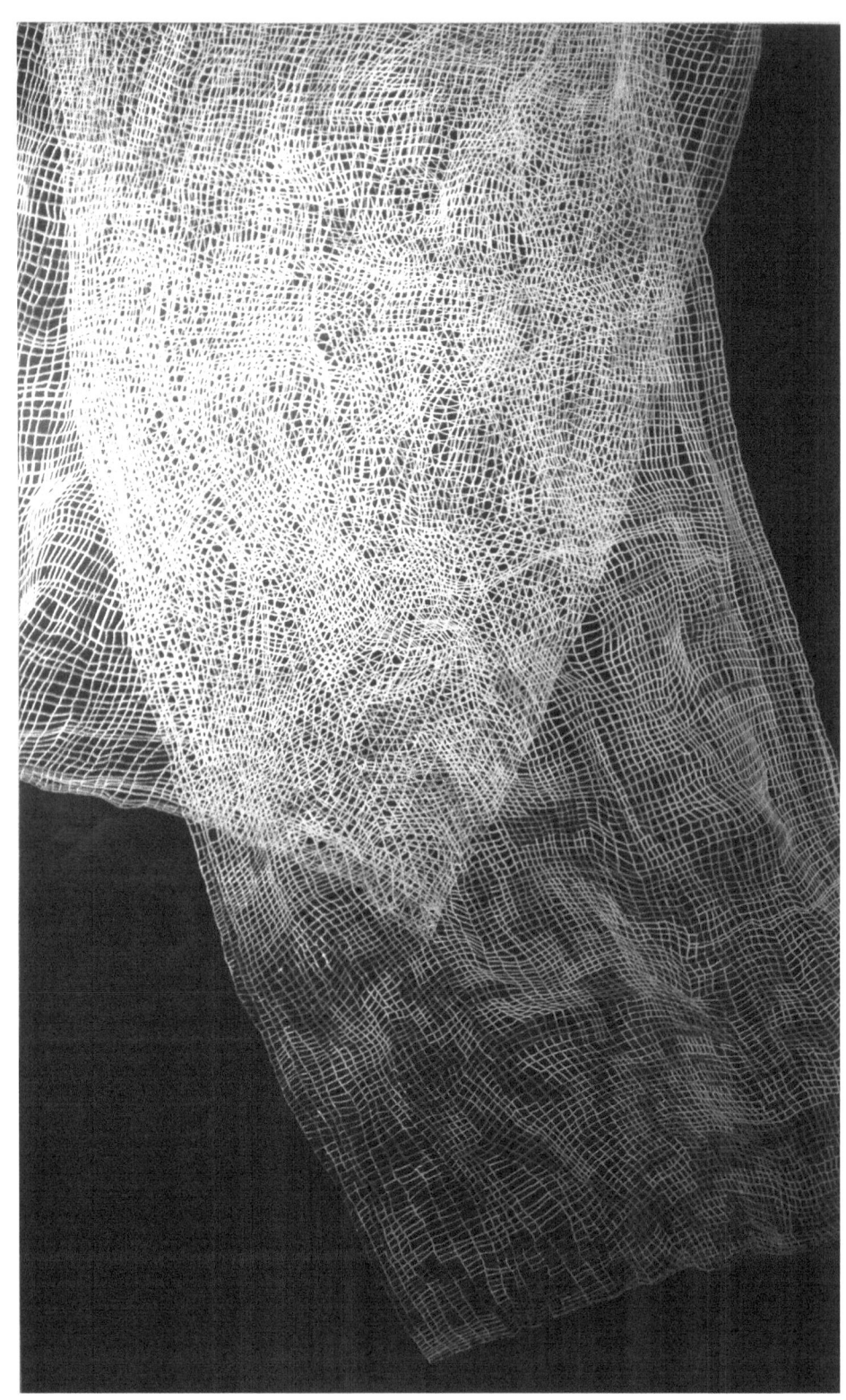

Untitled (Re-hung); 2016; Silver ink and acrylic on canvas; 60" x 36"

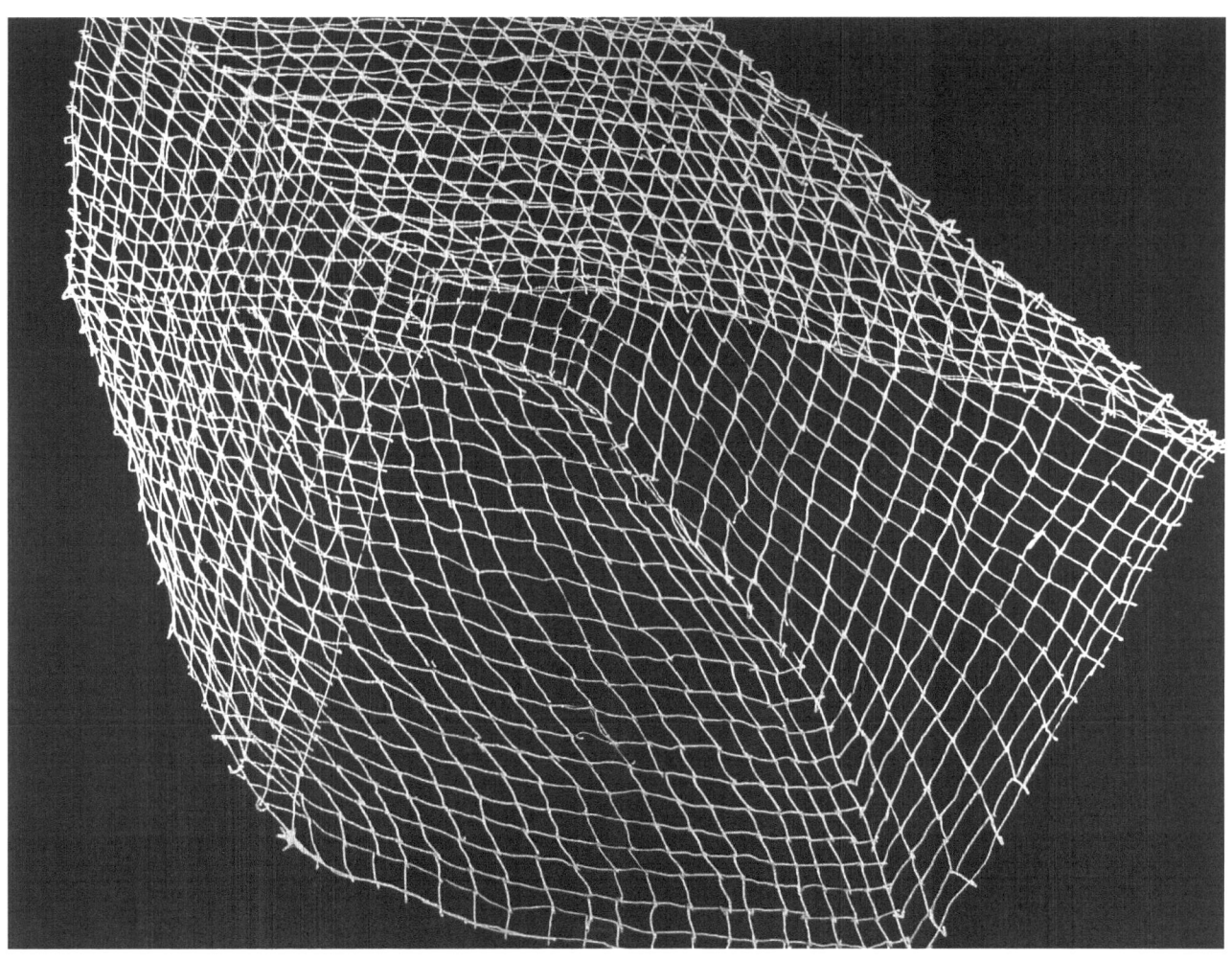

Untitled (Rabbit Cage 4); 2008; Silver ink and acrylic on panel; 9.5" x 12.5"

ABOUT

Caroline Burton received her MFA from Mason Gross School of the Arts, Rutgers and her BFA from The Cleveland Institute of Art. She has exhibited her work in NJ, NY, Oregon, Ohio, Tennessee and Massachusetts. She is the recipient of two New Jersey State Council on the Arts grants, three Geraldine R. Dodge Foundation grants, a Pollock-Krasner fellowship, and a grant from Rutgers Center for Print and Paper. Her work is included in many private and public collections throughout NJ and in the Dominican Republic.

"The process of organizing the unfamiliar is central to my sculpture, drawing and painting. My method, an intuitive one, has led to executions across several motifs including, architectural forms, the rabbit/pelt, the drain, the pillow, and the effects of accidents (personally and through art making). Linking them all is the context of a transformational process. Additionally, visual connection exists through the use of grid, which appears in nearly every piece, whether subtle or overt. Psychologically, the grid creates order and continuity as I traverse various themes." - C.B.

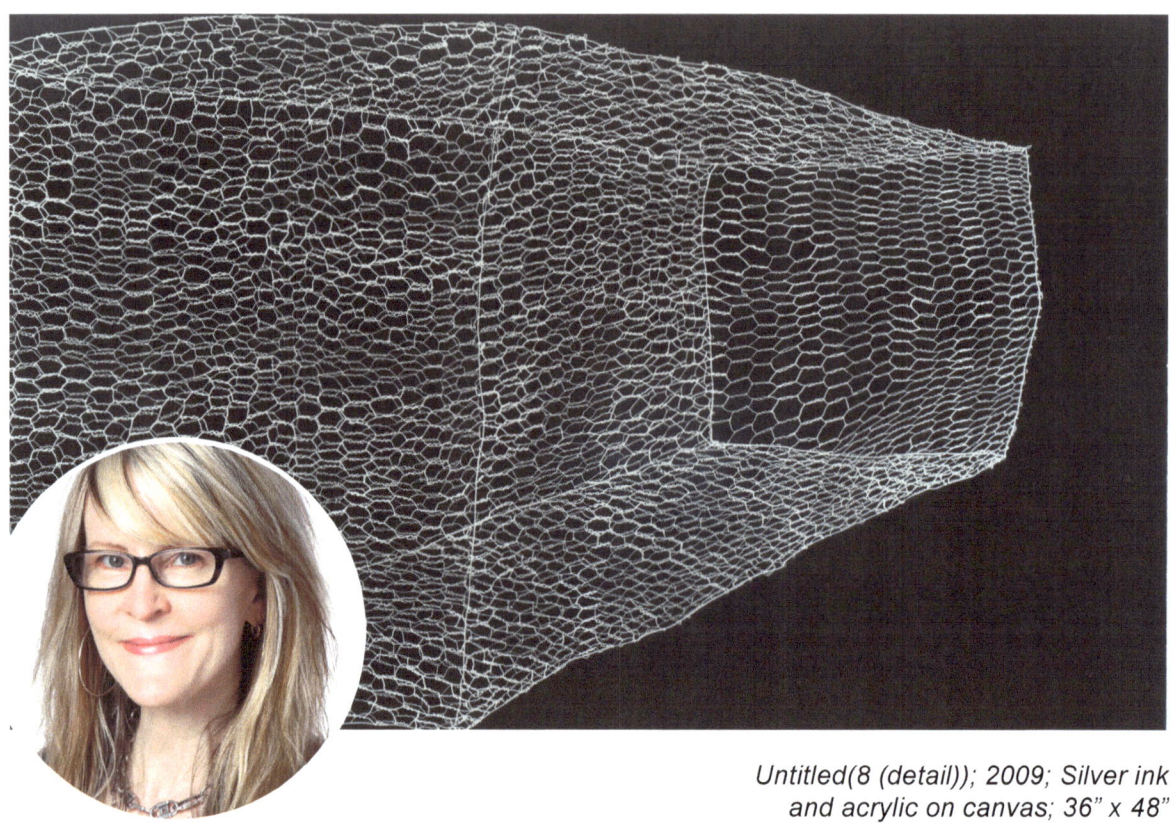

Untitled(8 (detail)); 2009; Silver ink and acrylic on canvas; 36" x 48"

DRAWING ROOMS INTERVIEW

DR: Please tell me about your work.
CB:*All of my work relates to the grid, though it can be hidden at times. My studio practice is an ongoing dialogue between the works I am making. All the work is interconnected psychologically or visually, though it is not necessarily obvious.*

DR: What got you interested in drawing?
CB: *I have made drawings as long as I can remember. Drawing is my means of documenting the world around me. I draw to interrogate what is going on in the studio, to create connections and to understand more deeply the work I am making.*

DR: What is your intention in making these drawings?
CB: *These drawings document sculpture and painting forms that are in process of being made. They capture the in-between stage. There is also a relationship to architecture, a long-standing interest of mine.*

DR: Where does your exploration with drawing take you?
CB: *It usually informs my next paintings or sculptural works, or it informs another body of drawings altogether. Drawing is the link between the works.*

DR: How is what you are drawing unique?
CB: *I think it may be unique due to the process behind it as I've explained here. (See above question about my intention).*

DR: Do you set up constraints or rules to follow? If so, do you stick to your rules or break them? Why or why not?
CB: *I try not to set up strict rules, but loose ones that can evolve over the course of making a work.*

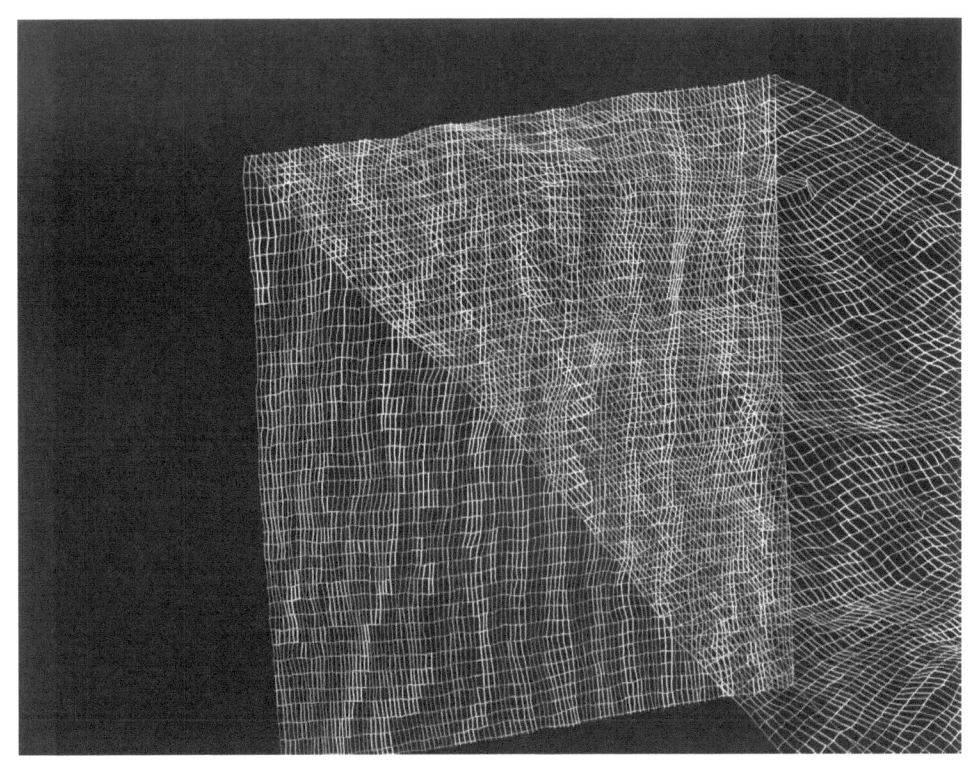

Untitled(10); 2009; Silver ink and acrylic on canvas; 36" x 48"

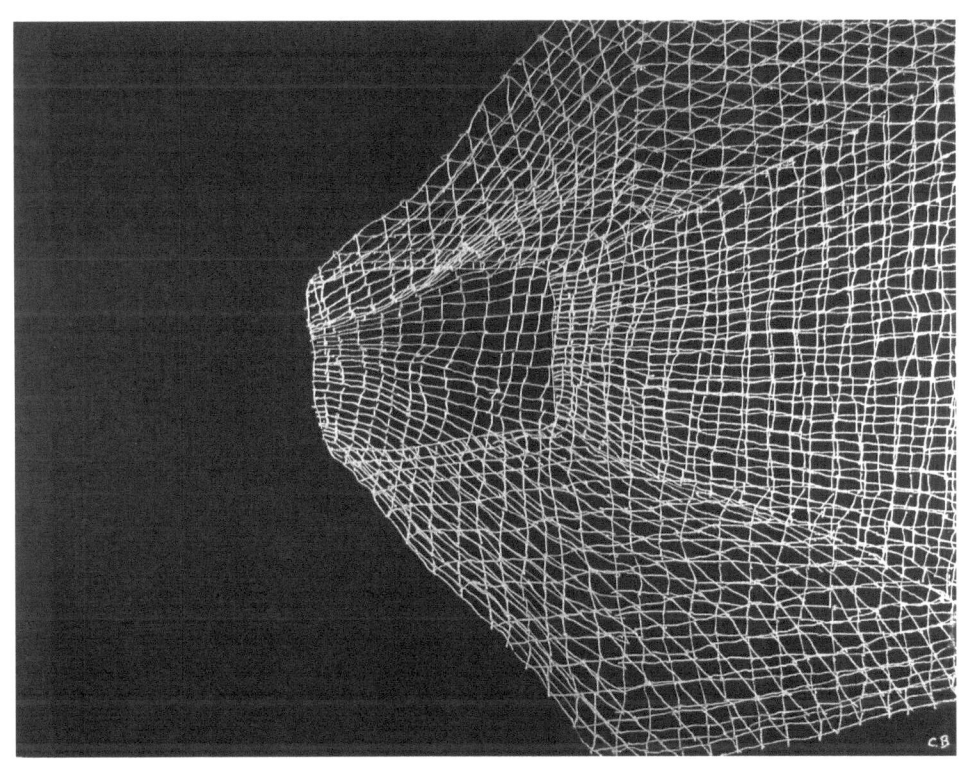

Untitled (Rabbit cage 3); 2008; Silver ink and acrylic on panel; 9.5" x 12.5"

HARRIET FINCK

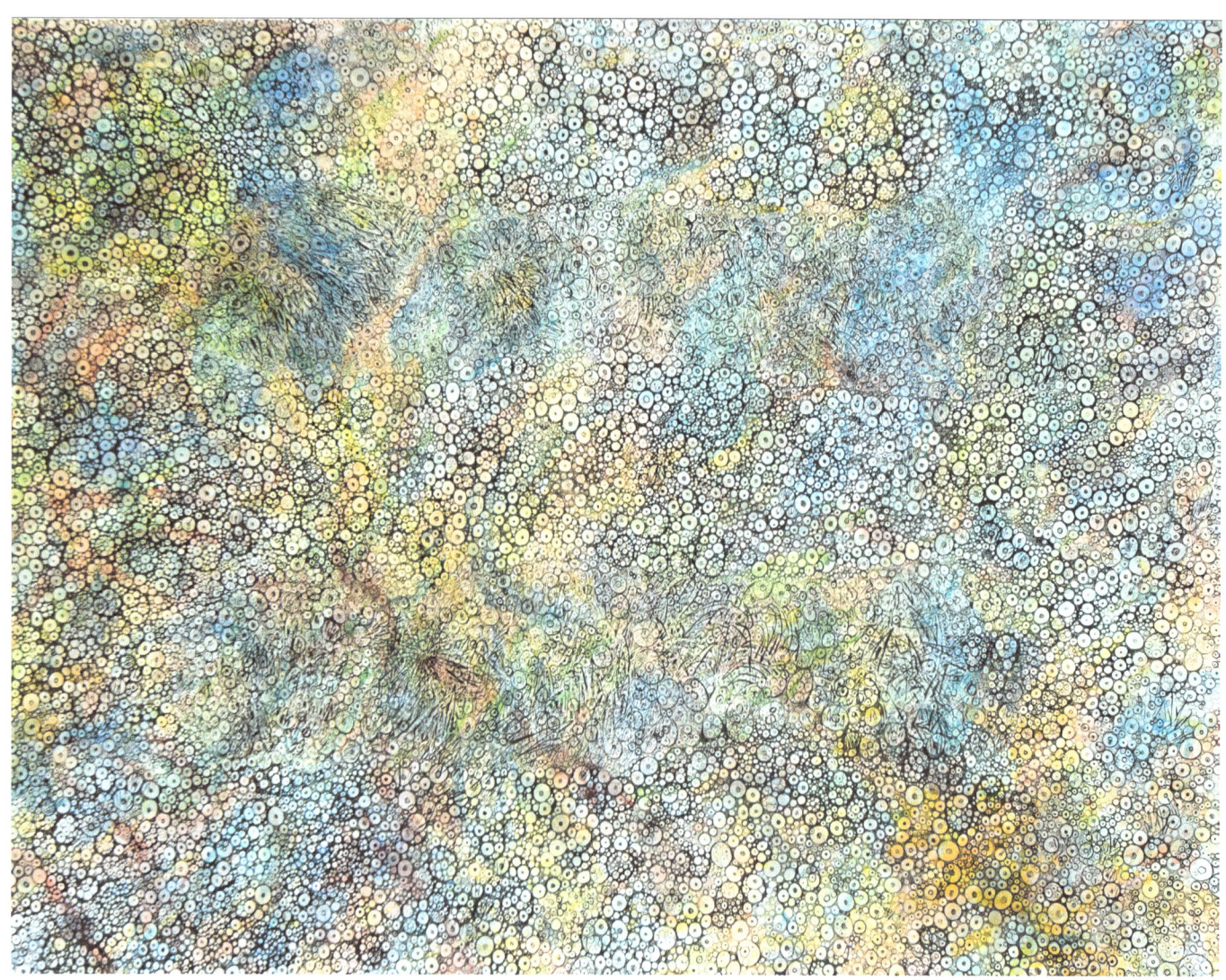

All the Rivers; 2016; Acrylic and ink on paper; 54" x 72"

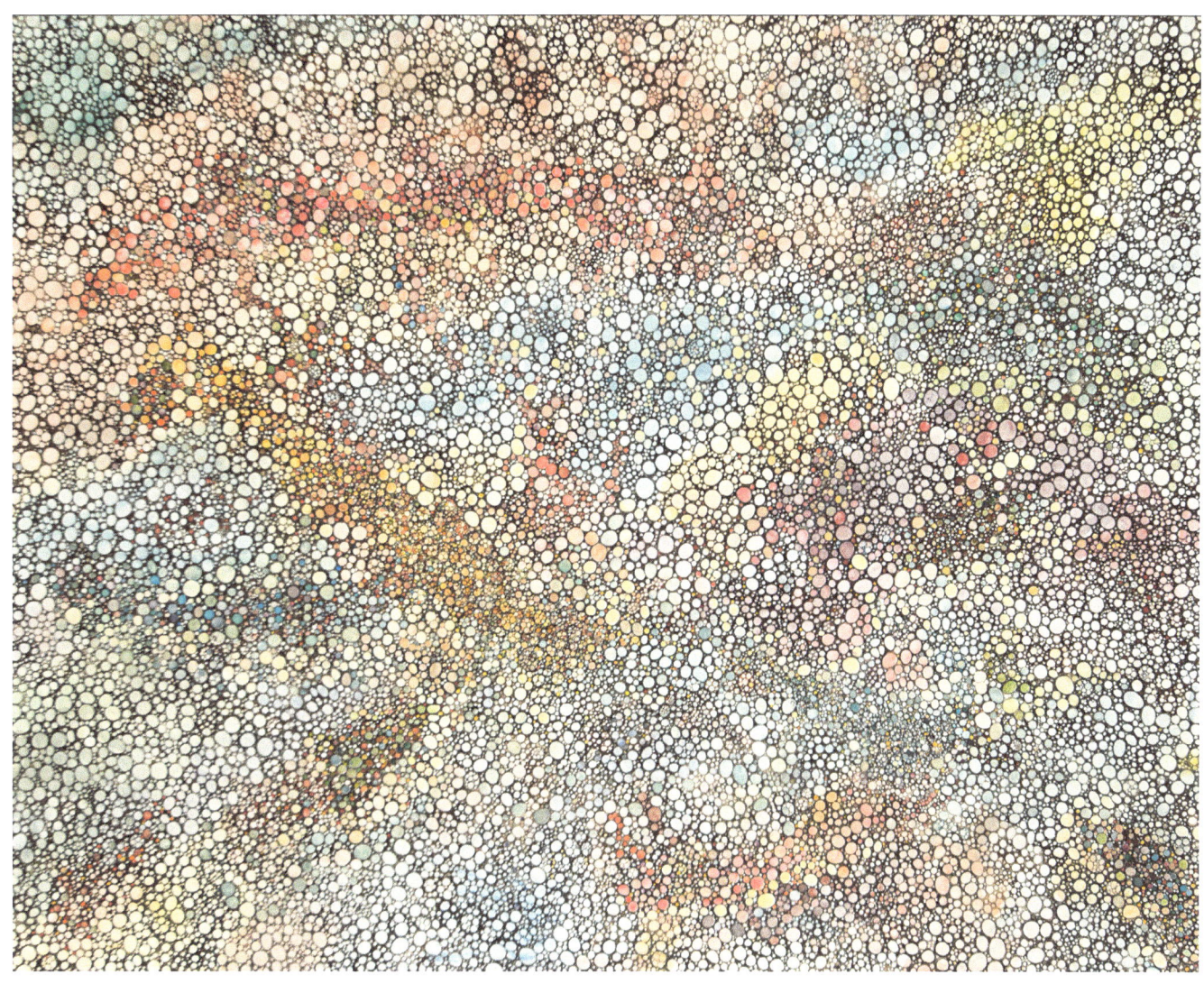

But the Sea is Never Full; 2016; Acrylic and ink on paper; 54" x 72"

ABOUT

Born in Brooklyn, raised in Queens, Harriet is a second generation American. In college she majored in art history and city planning, and in graduate school she studied architecture, received an M.Arch degree, and for many years worked as an architect. Harriet found her way back to art making through cutting up and reconfiguring her own etchings. Harriet teaches art at William Paterson and the Old Church Art Center.

"My work often straddles the border between painting and drawing. I work mostly on paper with a tiny crow quill pen and black ink. The subject of my work is repetitive patterns and rhythms of nature." - H.F.

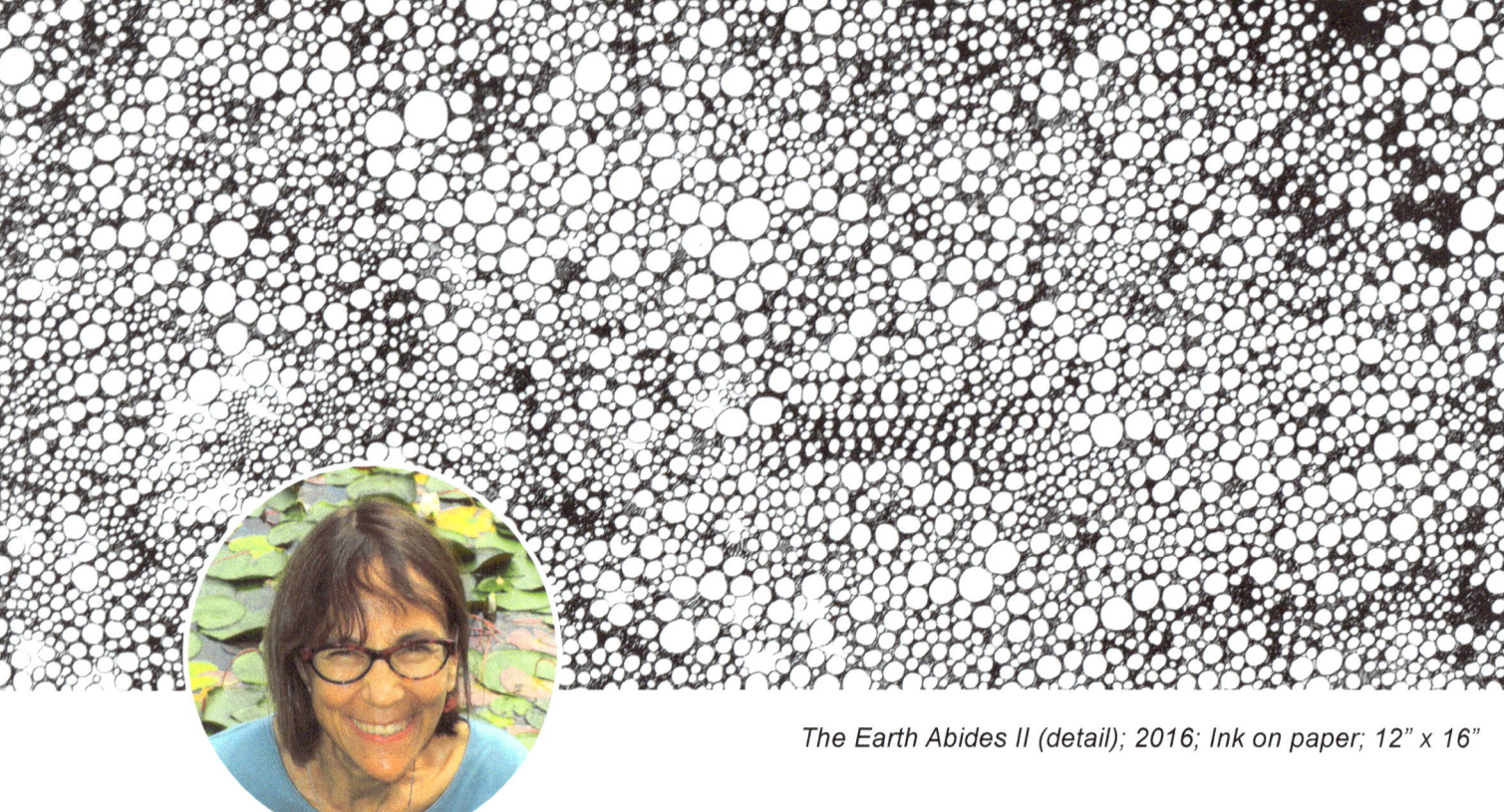

The Earth Abides II (detail); 2016; Ink on paper; 12" x 16"

DRAWING ROOMS INTERVIEW

DR: Please tell me about your work.
HF: I call it "organic abstraction". I'm interested in the micro/macro features of the universe. I like to play with old Hebrew texts about nature; they enrich my thinking; a touchstone.

DR: What got you interested in drawing?
HF: I've been drawing since I could hold a pencil. Drawing informs everything I do. I was an architect for many years. There, too, it was drawing that engaged me.

DR: What is your intention in making these drawings?
HF: I am interested in the repetition of small units that coalesce to become something bigger. For some of the drawings in this exhibit, this interest dovetails with the great theme in Ecclesiastes, which is about the circularity of time.

DR: Where does your exploration with drawing take you?
HF: It takes me into painting, and painting takes me back into drawing.

DR: How is what you are drawing unique?
HF: I don't know that it is unique, but I hope that it is true. I hope to be expressing something true about the nature of things.

DR: Do you set up constraints or rules to follow? If so, do you stick to your rules or break them? Why or why not?
HF: I use some simple words at the beginning, like "many" or "few", "tight " or "loose". I choose materials: paper, ink, a kind of paint. I choose a paper size. If I'm working from a text, I study it. I work in series, so the first one is the hardest to set up. I love constraints and rules, but I also like to break them.

DR: Anything else you want to add?
HF: For me, drawing into painting is a continuum. I often hold a paintbrush like a pencil. I work on paper, whether it is a drawing or a painting. Another continuum is writing into drawing. Words as visual marks. Letters into simple shapes. Simple shapes into words and sentences.

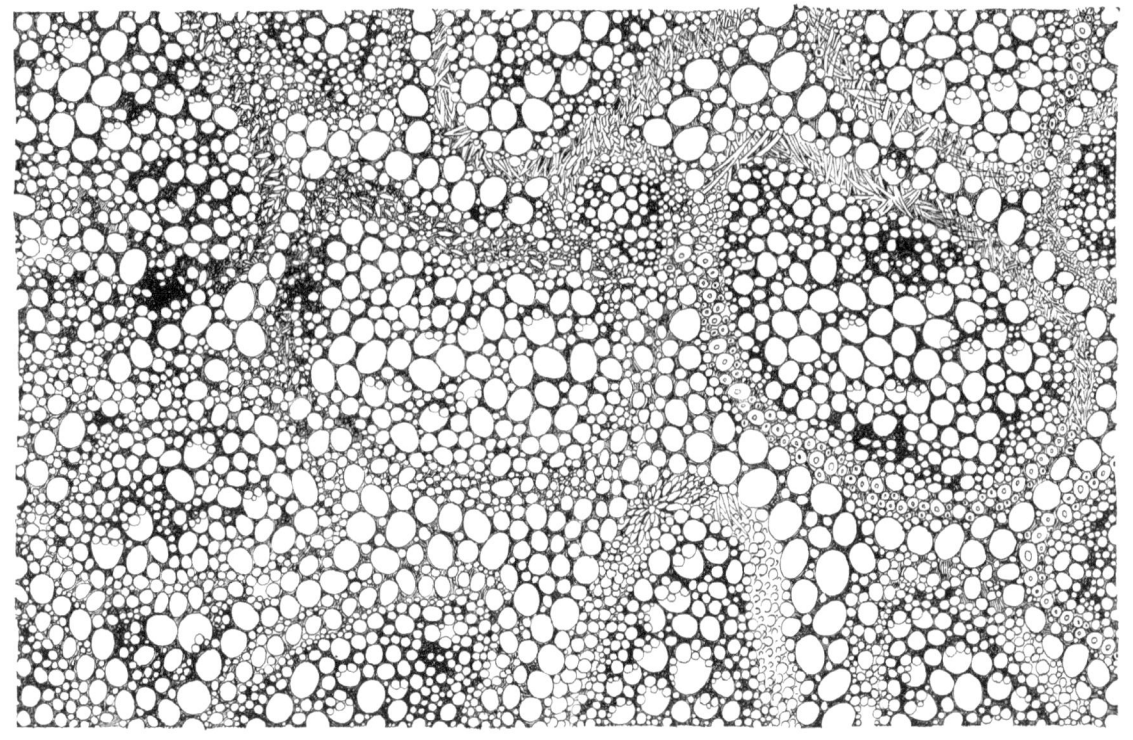

The Earth Abides I; 2015; Ink on paper; 12" x 16"

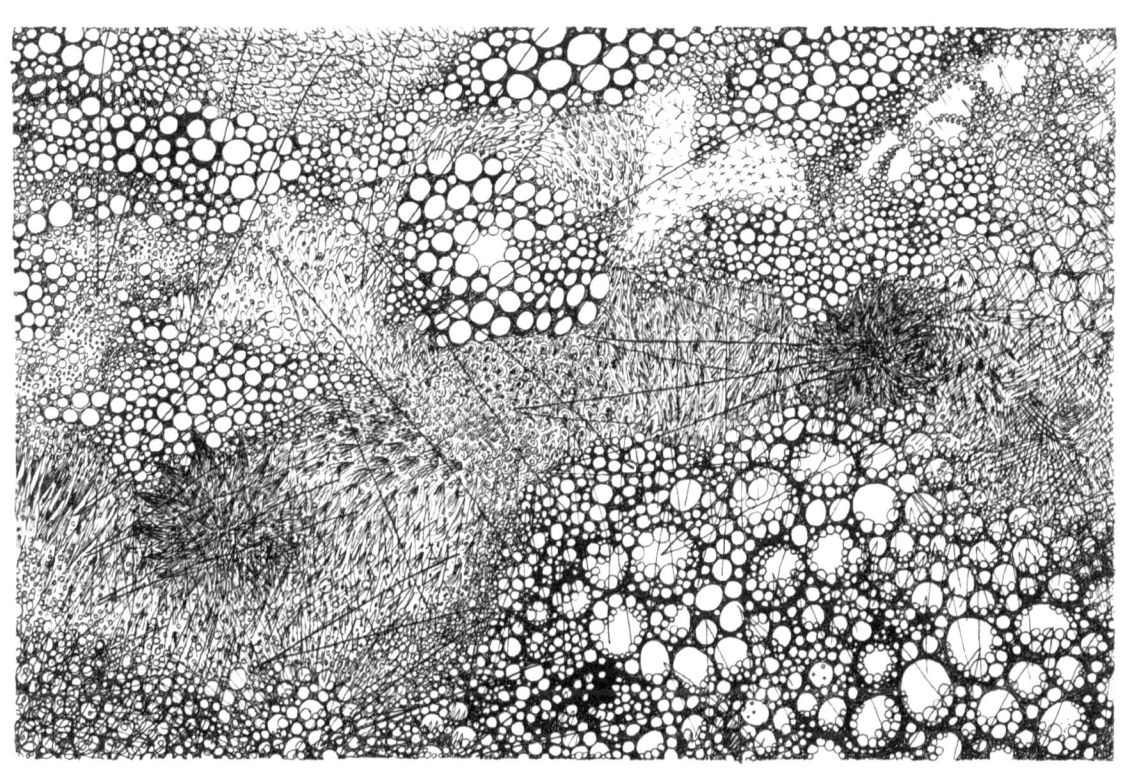

The Earth Abides IV; 2015; Ink on paper; 12" x 16"

HEEJUNG KIM

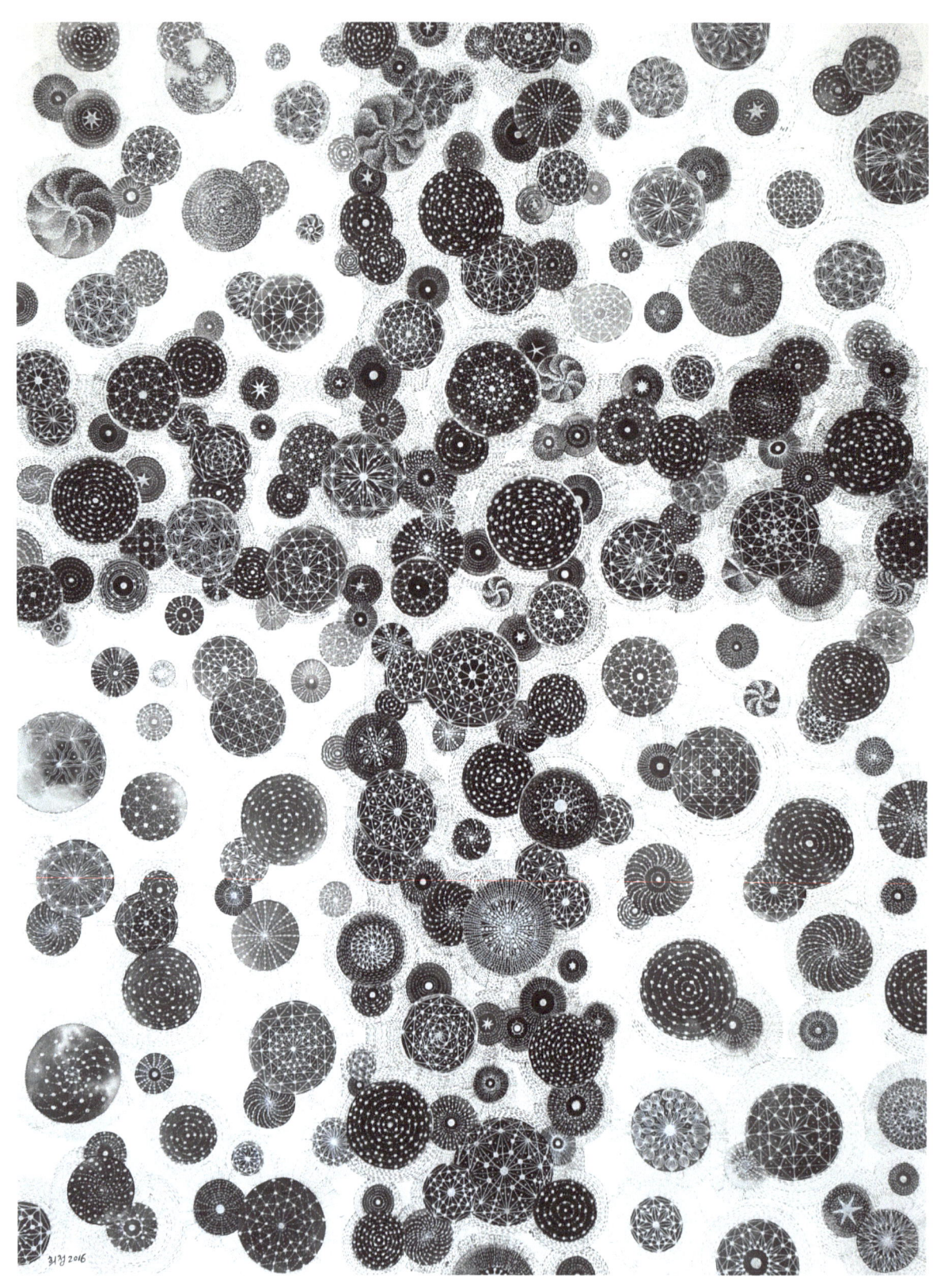

The Cross; 2016; Ink on paper; 17" x 23"

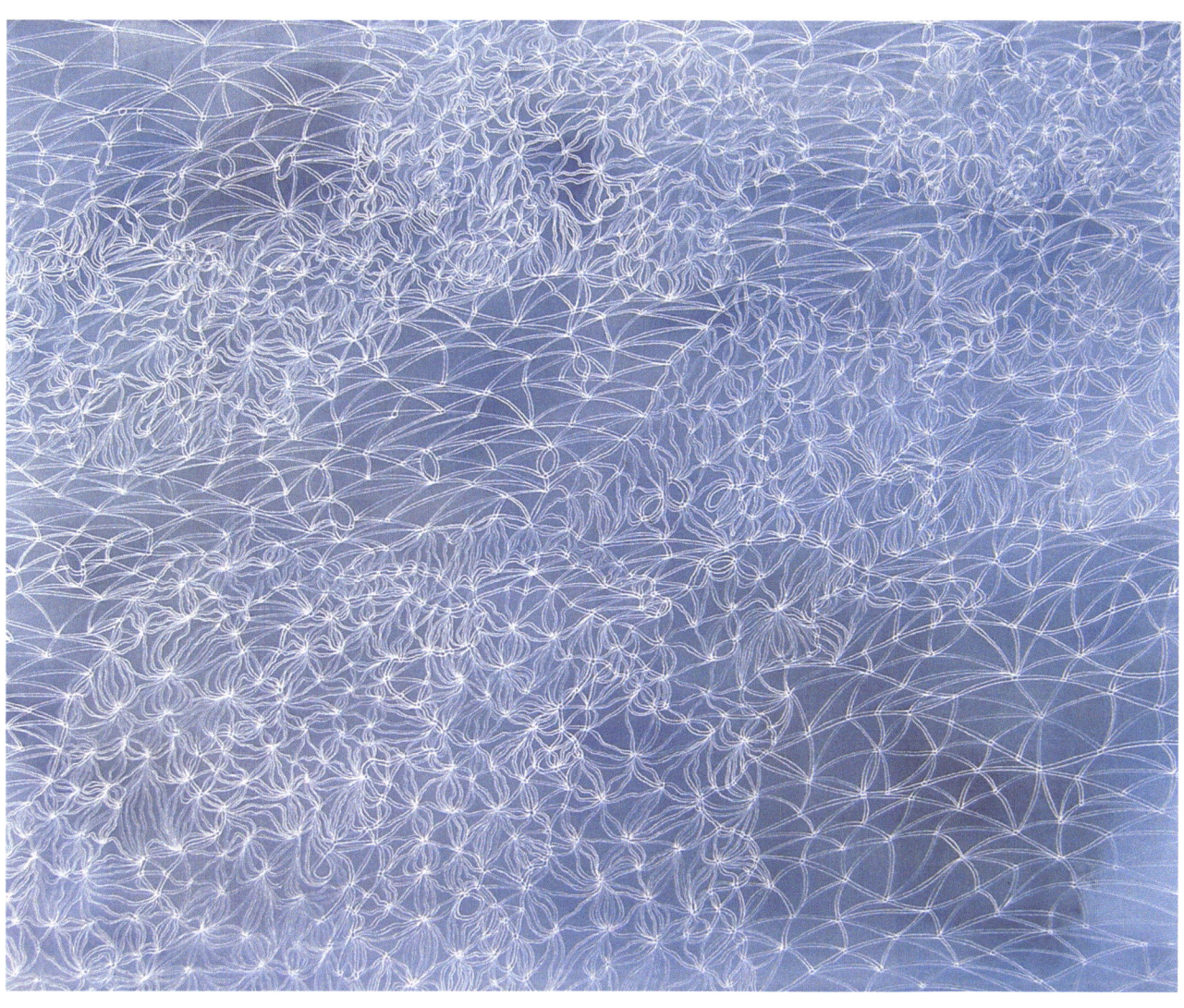

Karma 1; 2004; Ink on paper; 16" x 22"

ABOUT

Born in Seoul, Korea, Heejung Kim's work is inspired by her imagination and eastern philosophies, especially Buddhism. She obtained an MA in Art Education from the University of Illinois at Urbana-Champaign and an MFA from SUNY at Stony Brook. Heejung has had numerous exhibitions in NJ, NYC, Boston, Ohio and Oregon. Her work has been reviewed by ARTnews, The New York Times, The Star-Ledger and other publications. She has taught at New Jersey City University and the Raritan Valley Community College.

"My art works relate to a world that is not visible or tangible. Rather, the existence of this world is believed by people; it's the world between the living and the dead. My works contain images from the surreal, dreams, imagination, and religions, especially Buddhism. Similar to Buddhist monks who meditate upon Emptiness (one of the major doctrines in Buddhism), sitting on the same spot and facing the wall for days, months, or years, I repeat the same movement for hours and hours in order to complete my art works. While doing so, my mind becomes Empty, losing track of time, and eventually, the repetition of the same movement is transfigured as one of the methods for meditation." - H. K.

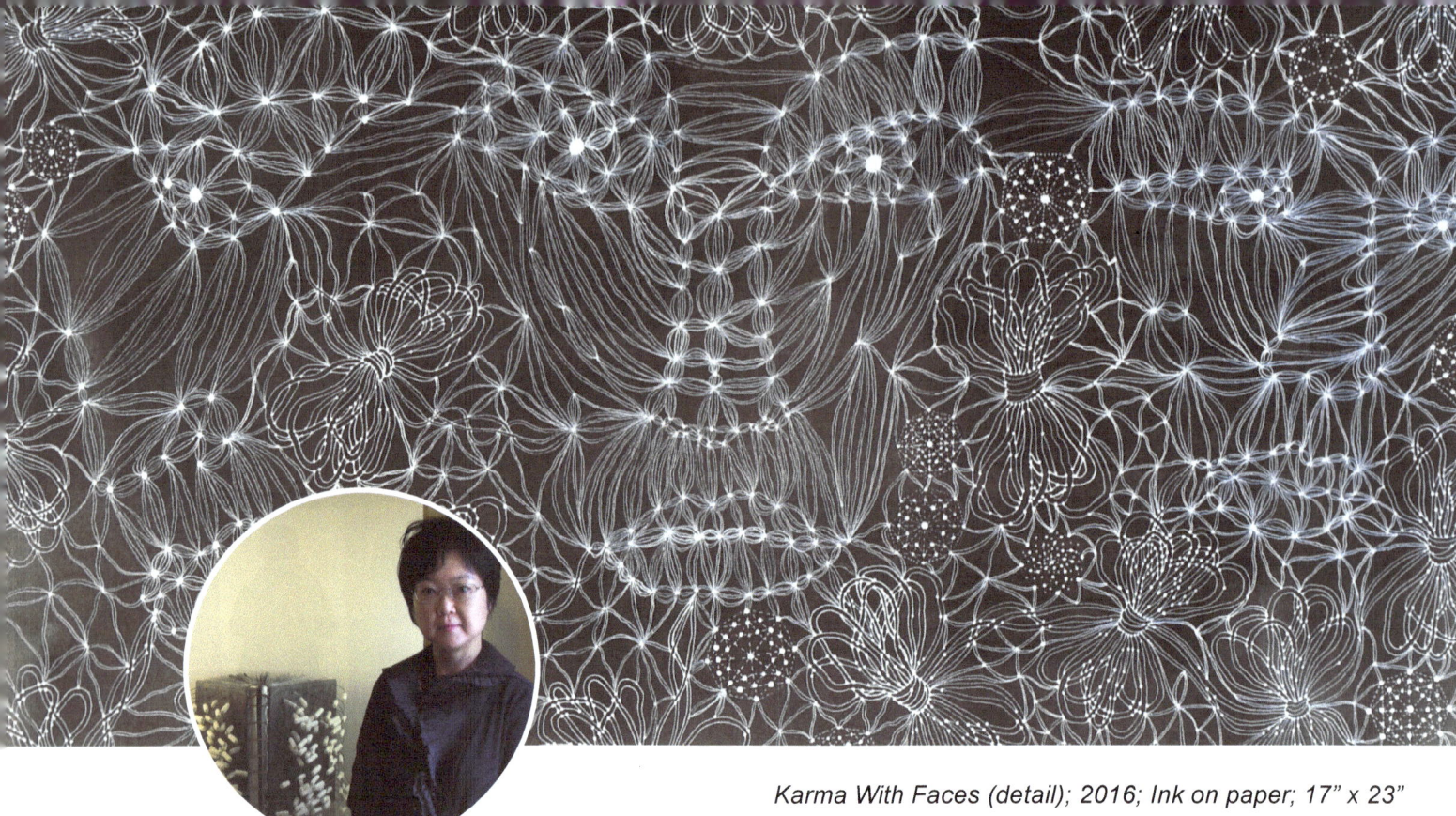

Karma With Faces (detail); 2016; Ink on paper; 17" x 23"

DRAWING ROOMS INTERVIEW

DR: Please tell me about your work.
HK: My work is inspired by Buddhism and the images in my dreams. I had the opportunity to study Tibetan Mandala paintings and I was fascinated by the patterns and symbols found in them. In my drawings, the concept of Karma plays an important role. It appears as the line that constantly meets and separates throughout the entire picture plane. That line represents the path of my life. I move to meet people, to stay, and at some point, to separate from them in many different ways. Often I try to combine this idea with the images in my dreams, my dream images. The most frequently appeared dream image is "Star in the Sky." I have loved stars in the sky since my childhood and had fun memorizing their names. Very often I dreamed that suddenly stars would come out and dance, like a festival and people would watch them dancing. In my work, my dream images are combined with the images found in the Buddhist Mandala.

DR: What got you interested in drawing?
HK: Drawing is a fundamental form of all other visual arts. I always do drawings before making artist books, sculptures, and paintings.

DR: What is your intention in making these drawings?
HK: I always question the border line between drawing and painting. Asians produce Asian paintings using ink with brush and we call them paintings. But in western common sense, when we see pen and ink as a medium, we easily consider it a drawing. My artwork stands between that border line, between drawing and painting.

DR: Where does your exploration with drawing take you?
HK: I keep making art using different images that appear one after the other in my mind. I usually don't know where I am going and what type of artwork it is going to be when I am through with a piece. It's like following my Karma. I am guided by my Karma now and I see that these works are heavily influenced by my previous Karma.

DR: How is what you are drawing unique?

HK: My drawing stands close to the border line between painting and drawing. I wet the paper with water, pour black ink, and let it dry. I add a little bit of intention to create certain shapes on the paper, then I start from the shape created by the natural force. I consider it as my Karma. I never wanted to be born as a woman and a Korean. It has been a restriction that I have had to deal with throughout my life. The pen drawing on top is my choice. I control and create anything on top of it. This process is related to my understanding of life. Now I am still a woman but I am a Korean-American.

DR: Do you set up constraints or rules to follow? If so, do you stick to your rules or break them? Why or why not?

HK: I do not set any rules intentionally when I produce art work, but certain processes and orders are always involved in my creating art. I cover or create a background, draw shapes using lines, and add color using markers, etc. I don't set a rule intentionally, but certainly order becomes a part of creating artwork and it's different in each case.

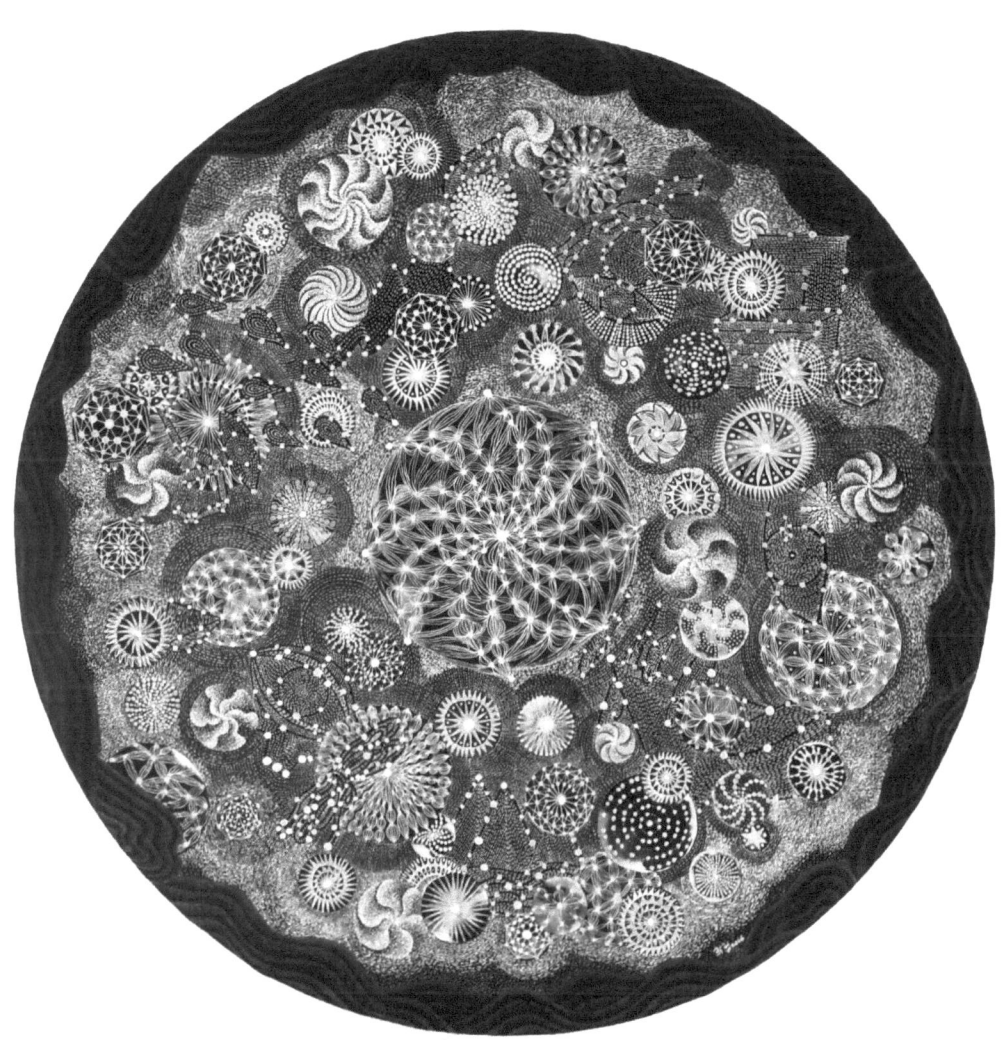

Dancing Star Mandala; 2016; Ink on paper; 17" x 23"

IBOU NDOYE

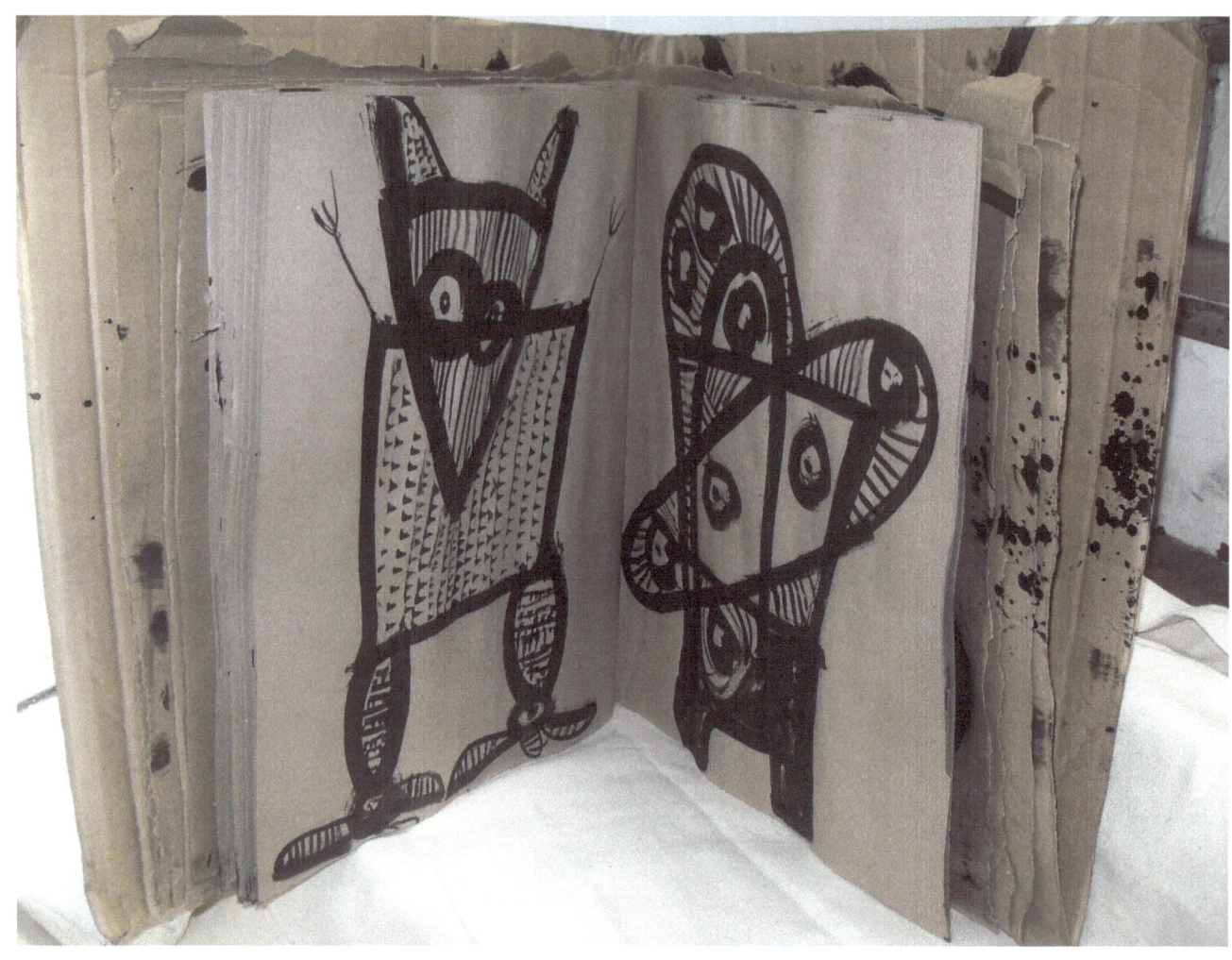

Black series # 1 (Book Art); 2010; Ink on Paper and cardboard (48 pages); 20" x 21"

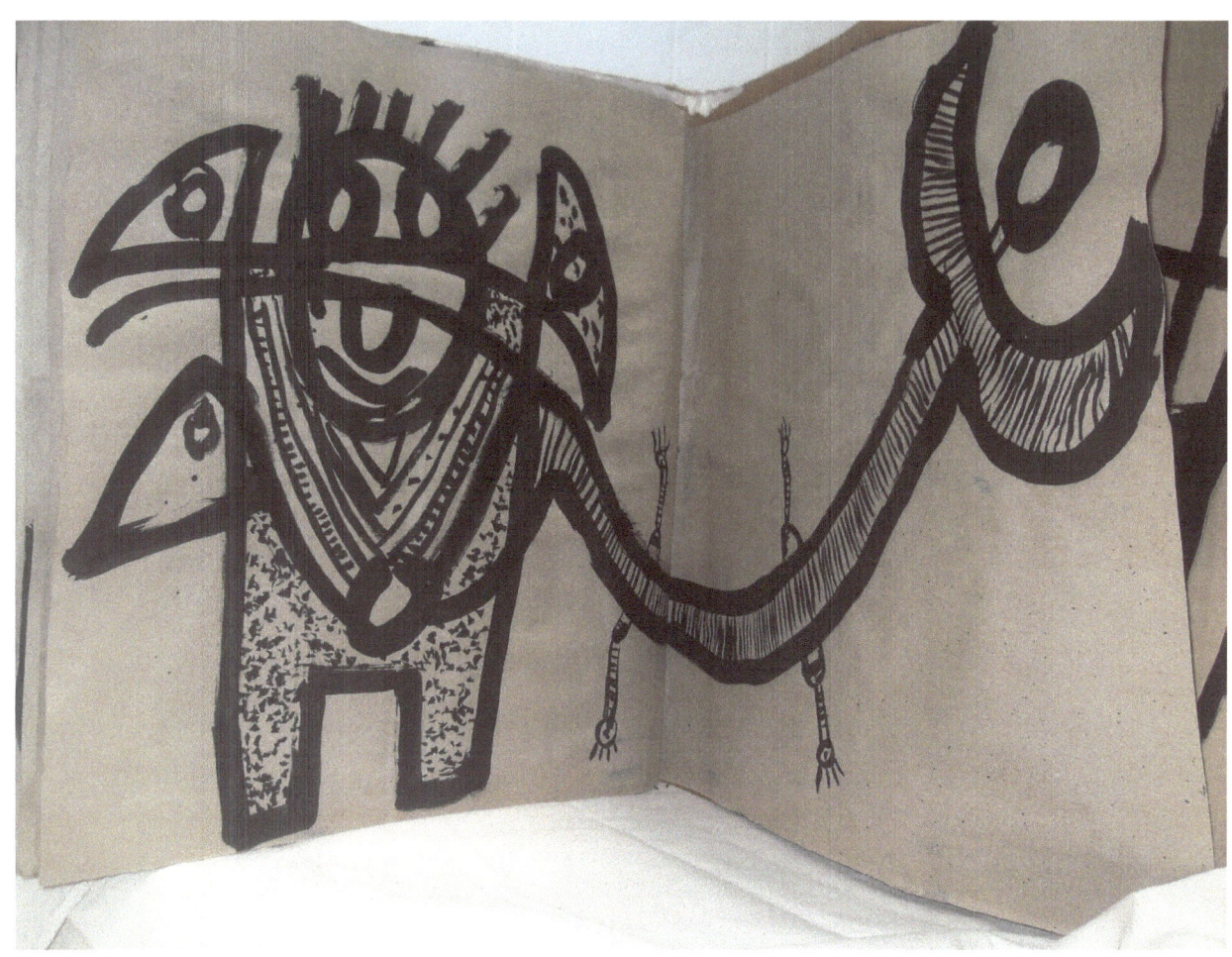

Black series # 2 (Book Art); 2010; Ink on Paper and cardboard (48 pages); 20" x 21"

ABOUT

Ibou Ndoye blends his West African culture with his immersion in urban life in the NYC/Jersey City area to produce art and narratives that are both relevant and rooted in his strong sense of artistic and social heritage. Born in Dakar, Senegal, he began his career there in the 1980s, painting murals and making paintings on glass as part of the Set Setal movement. After moving to the US in 2001, he continues an active presence, sharing his talent through exhibitions, workshops and classes in a wide variety of institutions including schools, museums, adult day care centers, homeless shelters and libraries from Brooklyn to Philadelphia. Ibou resides in Jersey City, and regularly exhibits his art both locally and internationally.

> *I am not an artist*
> *by intention or*
> *by choice or*
> *by training*
> *But, by birth*

"That is why, the means of communication I use in my art is an easy-to-understand or universal language. You would not need a dictionary, a large vocabulary or a translator to understand it, because it is 100% social, in the sense that it has a social function which allows it to deal with all the social ethics of modern and traditional life. It is the short story from an oral tradition that teaches, informs, awakens, communicates, and commits you to the cause of answering the unasked questions of people with facial expressions. My art can also be regarded as the channel through which people watch themselves acting alive or pre-recorded." - I.N.

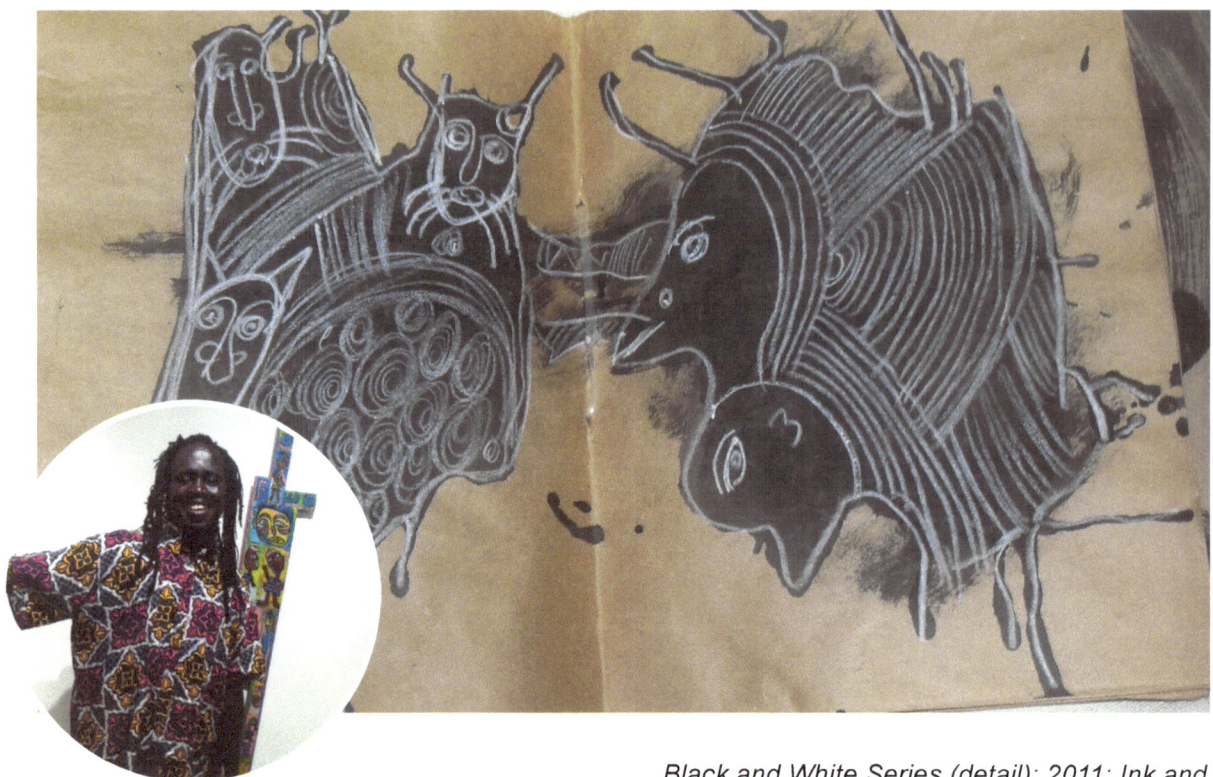

Black and White Series (detail); 2011; Ink and acrylic pencil on paper and cardboard; 10" x 12"

DRAWING ROOMS INTERVIEW

DR: Please tell me about your work.
IN: My works on paper are strong line drawings with ink on heavy kraft paper. I just let my hands slide on the paper and pour out what is in my memory. I sometimes challenge myself while drawing by using my left and right hands. I do not want to erase anything.

DR: What got you interested in drawing?
IN: I have always been interested in drawing. As a child I saw my mother sketching dresses or skirts for her customers after having listened to their explanations and descriptions and also grandmother drawing patterns on fabric for her needle work.

DR: What is your intention in making these drawings?
IN: To make a fast and detailed drawing non stop for one hour on a big piece of paper. I was trying to quickly tell stories that caught my eyes in a specific moment and place.

DR: Where does your exploration with drawing take you?
IN: My explorations with drawings are limitless. I draw on anything I can lay my hand on. I also experiment with the medium I draw. For example, the pages of one of the books was wet when I was drawing on it.

DR: How is what you are drawing unique?
IN: They are unique because when draw, I rejuvenate and act younger than my age, and I try to fuse my experience in Africa and America.

DR: Do you set up constraints or rules to follow? If so, do you stick to your rules or break them? Why or why not?
IN: I do not have rules when I draw. Rather, I feel like a blind man with walking stick who just fumbles until he reaches where he wants to be.

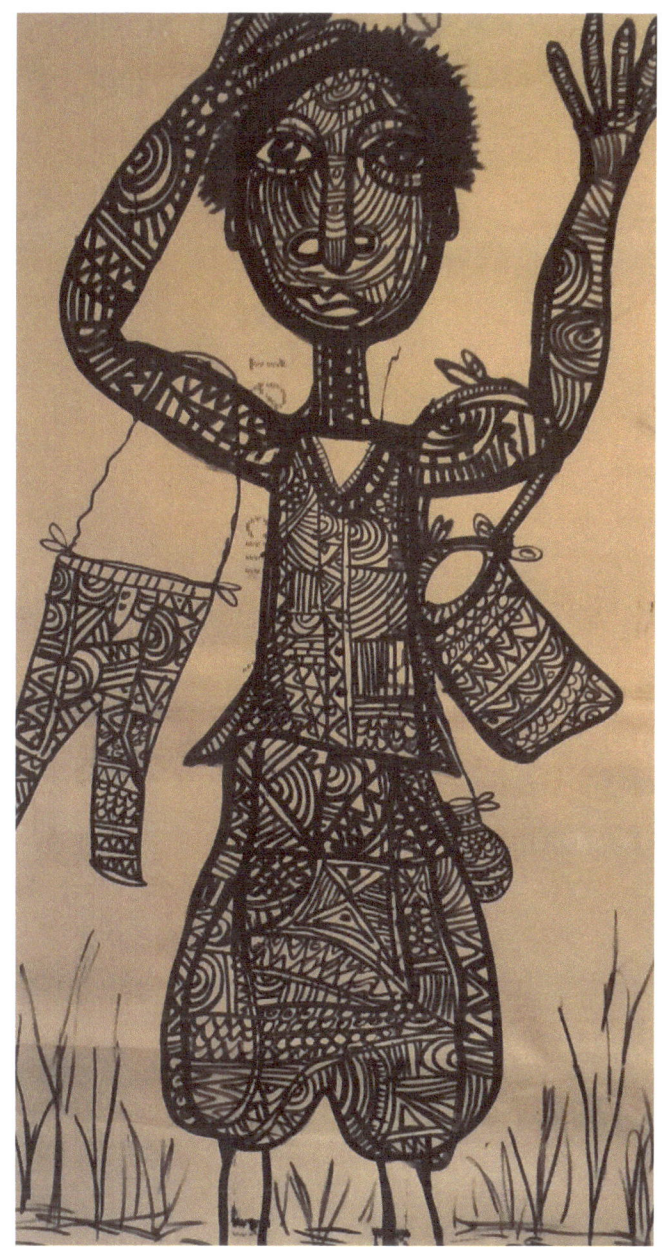

Lost Boy; 2016; Ink on Paper; 42" x 78"

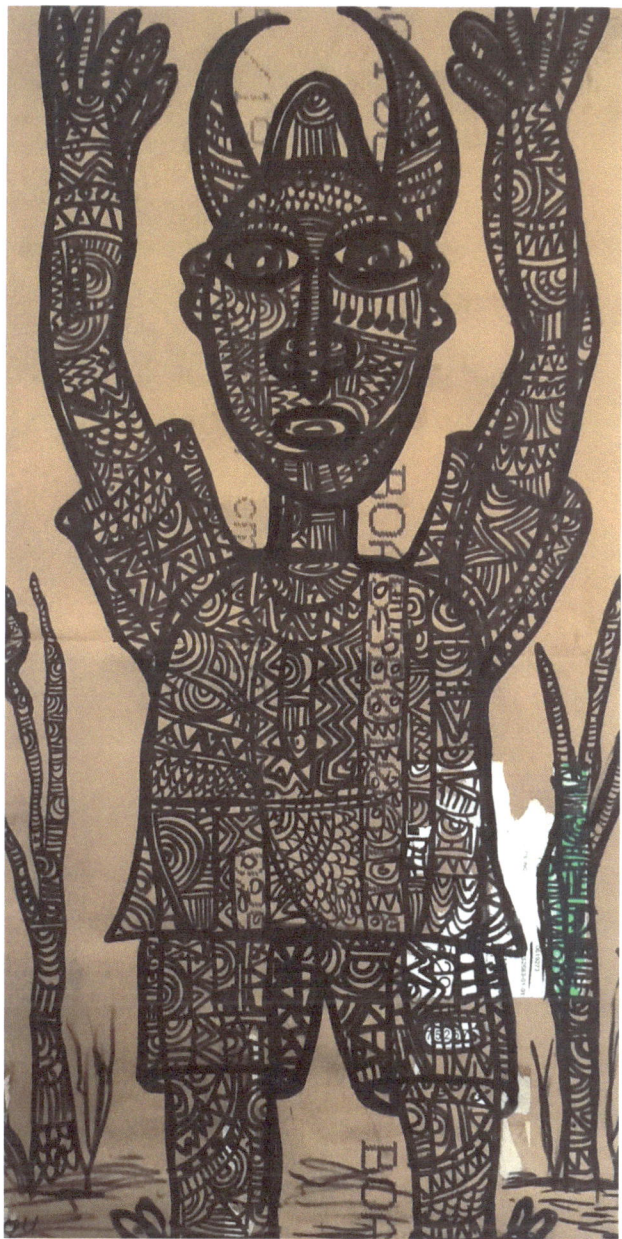

I am Living Mask; 2016; Ink on Paper; 42" x 78"

JOSEPH GERARD SABATINO

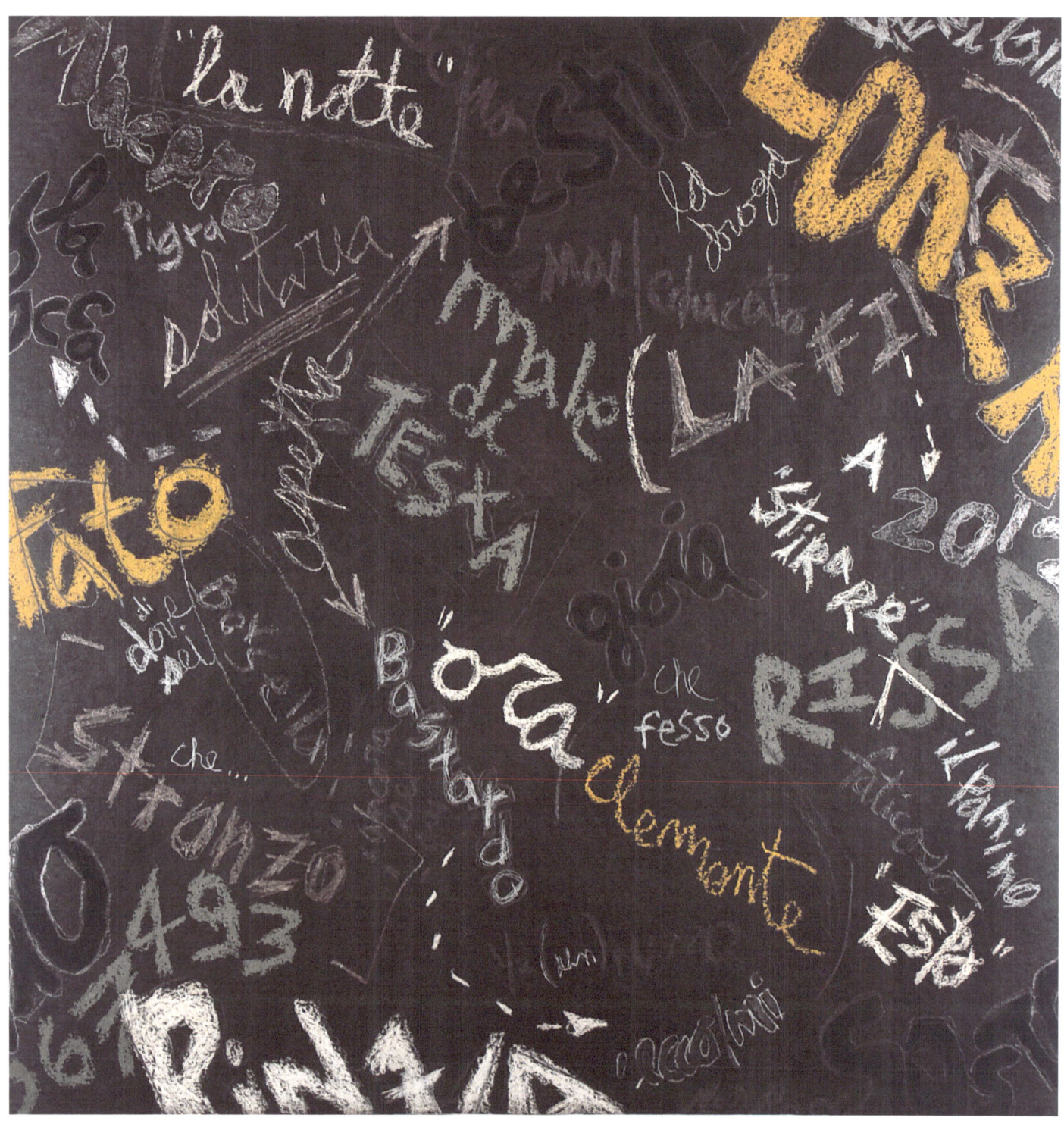

Lonza; 2011; Mixed Media on asphalt paper; 36.25" x 36.25"

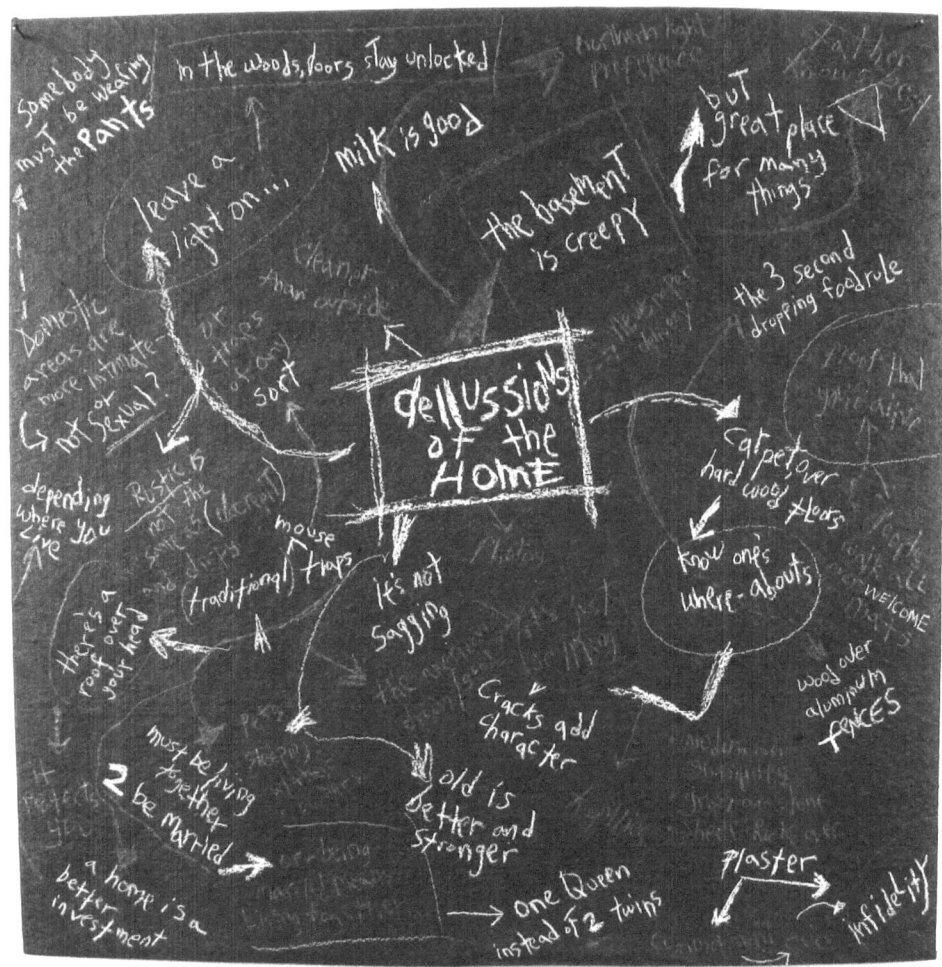

Dellusions of the Home; 2008; Mixed Media on asphalt paper; 21.5" x 21.5"

ABOUT

Joseph Gerard Sabatino was born in Belleville, NJ and maintains a studio in Paterson, NJ. Beginning as a photographer, he received a BA in Fine Art Studio from Montclair State University. He was a recipient of Aljira's 'Emerge' Artist Fellowship and the William and Dorothy Yeck Award for Miami University's "National Young Sculptors Competition." He has shown his work in the NY metropolitan area as well as internationally, in Italy and Austria. His work has been written about in The New York Times and ArtVoices Magazine. He participated in Deltarte's Artist Residency Program in Veneto, Italy.

"My drawing materials generally include black fabric dyes, ink, charcoal, oil sticks, wax, string, graphite and white/silver welder's pencils. Unrestricted and spontaneous, the drawings are all expressed with an immediate impulse to release a vigorous amount of energy in the least amount of time" - J.G.S.

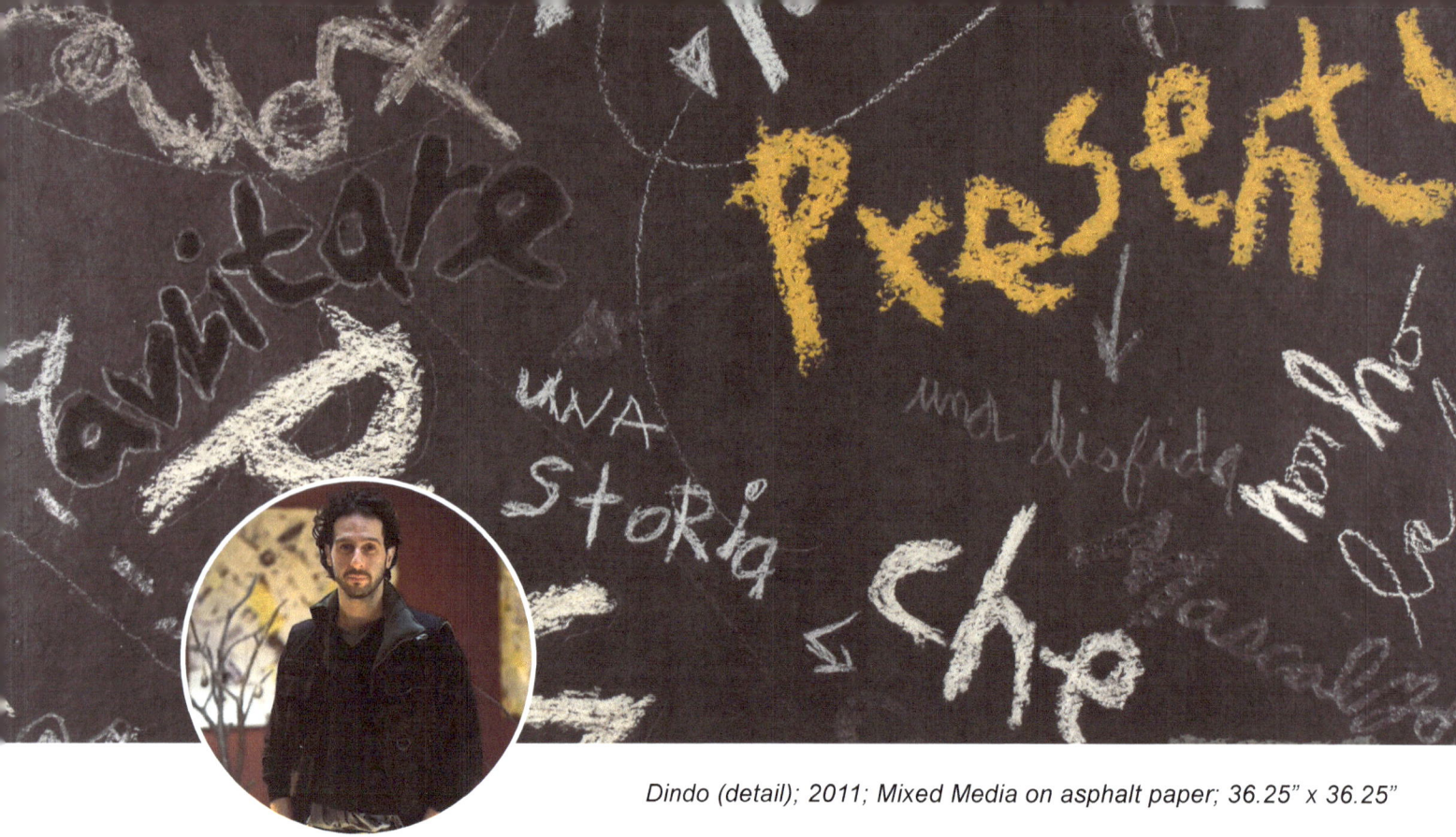

Dindo (detail); 2011; Mixed Media on asphalt paper; 36.25" x 36.25"

Photo by Studio Pic II

DRAWING ROOMS INTERVIEW

DR: Please tell me about your work.
JGS: I work in mixed media sculpture, installation and works on paper. In 2001, I returned to fulfill my final semester at Montclair State University after studying a semester abroad at Lorenzo de' Medici Institute of Art in Florence, Italy. Upon the completion of my last independent study course in photography, I decided that would be the last time I would use the medium as my main, sole chosen form. The body of work I produced in Italy was paired with the timely freedom of the independent study. The two separate experiences fused and naturally allowed for personal, professional and artistic awareness. The systematic flexibility to expand in a multifaceted approach to art making became instinctive by default.

DR: What got you interested in drawing?
JGS: I was always attracted to the immediate physicality and brute force needed to convey a gesture with various primitive tools of the trade. Drawing has always been an act, an action that at times can be physically painstaking and daunting depending on the scale and technique. I love to see how impulsive lines and pressures react to different surfaces and instruments. Drawing has always been a way to warm up my mind and body to convey the primal core of that moment. Drawing is a register of time, a formal documentation of being, a human seismograph machine or electrocardiogram graphic validating a whiplash of movements.

DR: What is your intention in making these drawings?
JGS: Initiated in 2005 from the Passages series while at The Jentel Foundation Residency Program, these works were done in isolation in Banner, WY where the land was open and stark, the night was pitch black and there was an absence of civilization. I decided to keep my door sealed anytime I was there and asked for no interruptions. I lined the walls with asphalt paper and began visually recording time. The process started with hash marks that indicated the days that I confined myself. With nothing but pacing and the observation of emptiness, the associated layers began to take shape.

DR: Where does your exploration with drawing take you?

JGS: I usually like to sweat when I work on my drawings; that's when I know I've reached a good point in the process. On the contrary, the Italian inspired text panels from the, "Aroma di Roma" series and "Passages," relied on a dialogue of internal and external exchanges. My surroundings and environments had to be captured, processed and sealed. At a later time, they needed to be transferred in their new form and choice of everyday supplies onto two dimensional surfaces. The Italian words found within Dindo or Lonza are terms coined from day to day conversations while absorbing the sights and sounds of Rome's urban sprawls.

DR: How is what you are drawing unique?

JGS: I use a host of industrial materials to mimic things that may typically look traditional. One may think they are observing a specific material until they realize it's a completely foreign object or form.

DR: Do you set up constraints or rules to follow? If so, do you stick to your rules or break them? Why or why not?

JGS: I don't want to think at all, my drawings require the freedom to be loose. They're reactionary, raw and immediate impulses, whether expressed physically, visually or mentally.

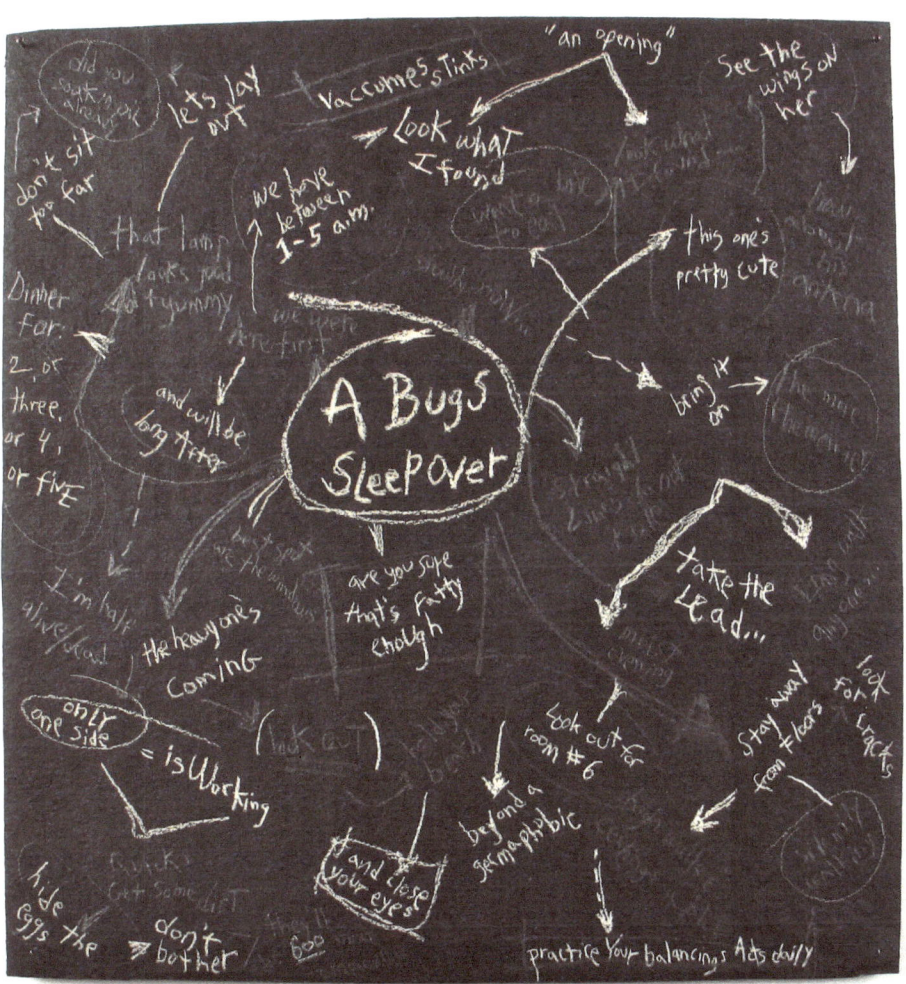

A Bug's Sleep Over; 2008; Mixed Media on asphalt paper; 21.5" x 21.5"

MARSHA GOLDBERG

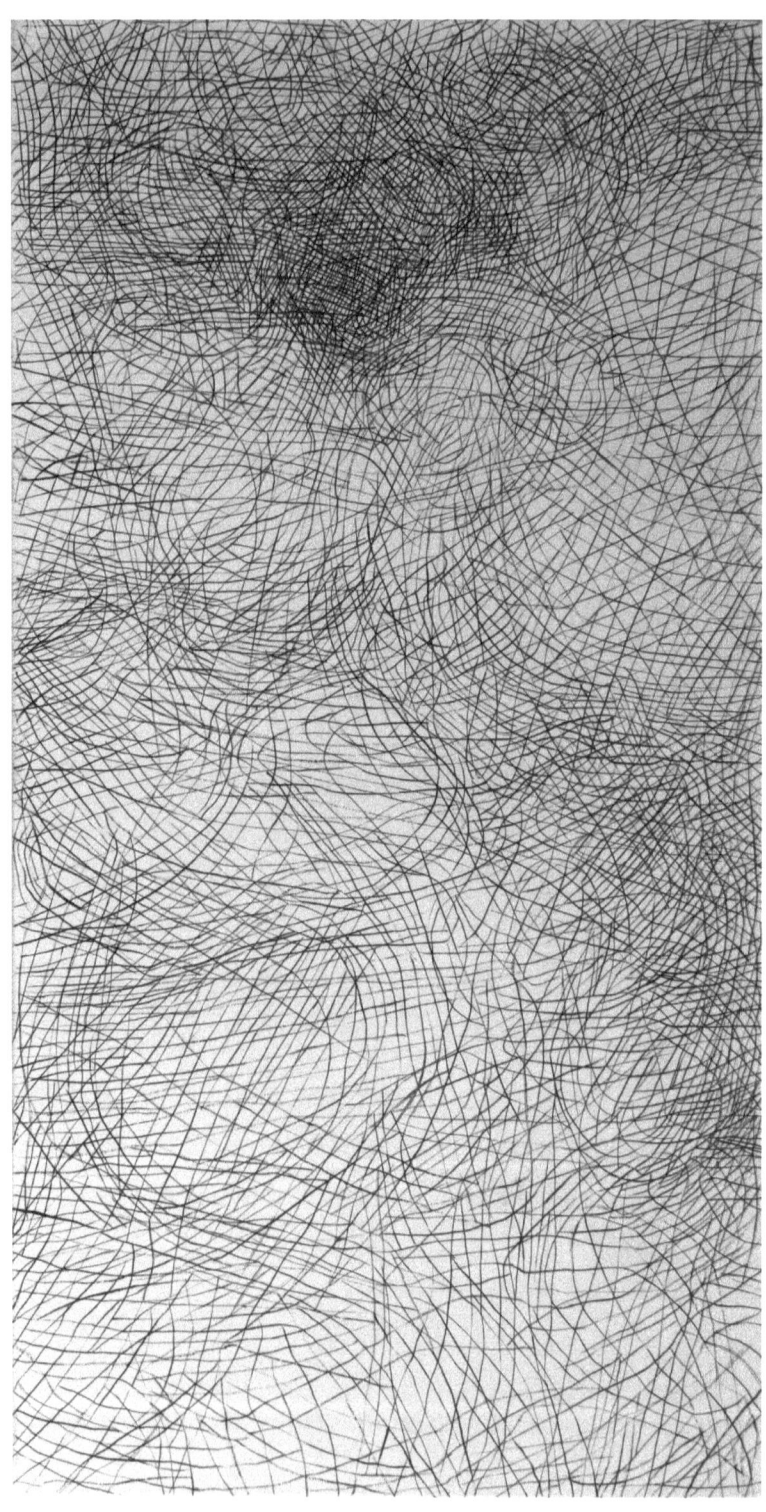

*Smoke Rises Traces #15; 2013; India
ink on gessoed canvas; 25" x 13"*

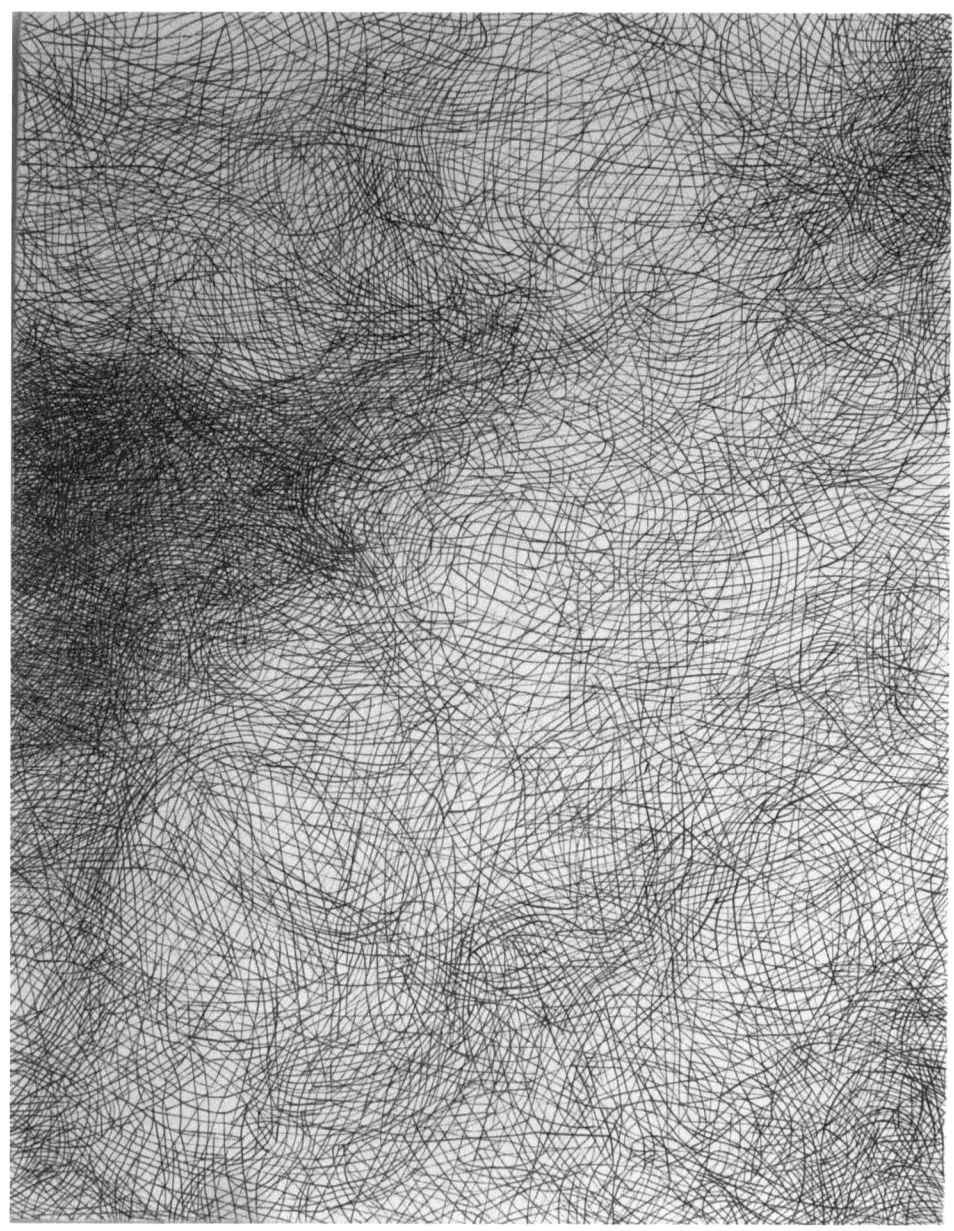

Smoke Rises: Traces #17; 2013; India ink on gessoed canvas; 24" x 19"

ABOUT

Marsha Goldberg is an artist who lives and works in Highland Park, NJ. Originally from Boston, she has also lived in Tucson, AZ, and in Jerusalem, Israel, and her travels have taken her to Southeast Asia, Europe, and the Middle East. Marsha's work has been exhibited widely and is included in the collections of Harvard University's Fogg Art Museum and the Boston Public Library.

"Captions accompanying war imagery in news media are often unintentionally poetic ("Smoke Billows From Houses On The Syrian Side"). The act of making contemplative art based on violent events is similarly paradoxical. This group of drawings is based on news photographs of war-related explosions. The meticulously made graphite drawings are directly sourced from the photos, omitting details that refer to location or scale. An explosion is loud, and sudden. Learning of violent events by means of still photographic images is misleading. These drawings may seem to be "realistic," but in what ways do they really represent war at all?" - M. G.

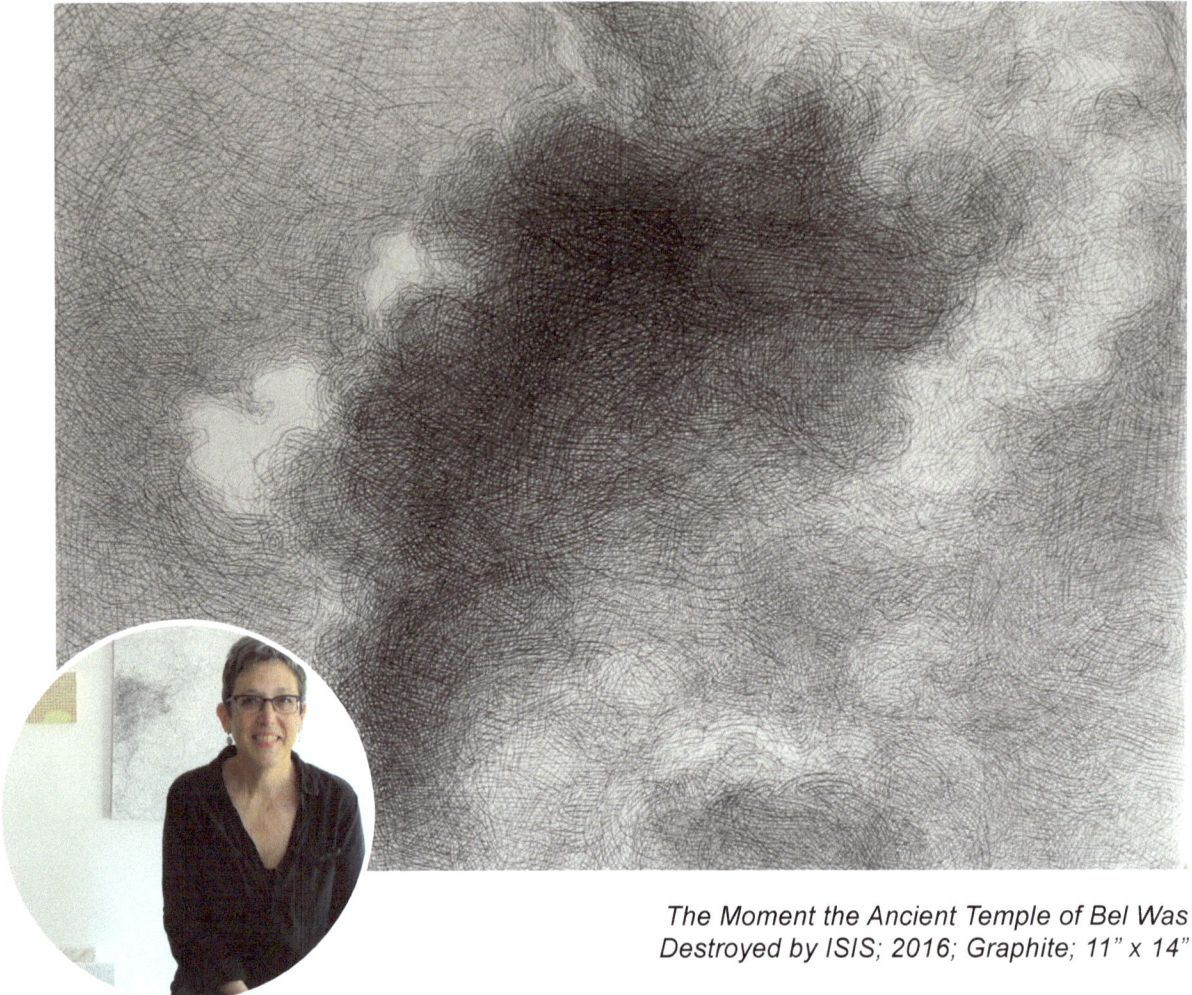

The Moment the Ancient Temple of Bel Was
Destroyed by ISIS; 2016; Graphite; 11" x 14"

DRAWING ROOMS INTERVIEW

DR: Please tell me about your work.
MG: There are two groups of drawing I'll be contributing. The graphite drawings on paper describe news photographs of smoke that results from war-related explosions. The images contain only the forms of the smoke, no other details, and the process is an accumulation of intersecting lines. Ink-on-gessoed canvas drawings make up the other group, which are based on small details of the graphite drawings. By enlarging and cropping these details, I shift my focus from the news image to the way my own drawings are made, further from the real event toward a contemplation of art-making and my process.

DR: What got you interested in drawing?
MG: Drawing has always been an integral part of my studio practice, in its own right and as a way to work out ideas related to paintings.

DR: What is your intention in making these drawings?
MG: I think of these drawings as a means to consider the ubiquitous images of war as presented in the media. They are about the photographs as much as they are about the events that are photographed. The fact that my methods are slow, careful and contemplative, in contrast to the violent events that they describe, is of interest to me.

DR: Where does your exploration with drawing take you?
MG: Drawing always makes me look more carefully. It is also a means of thinking about whatever the content is, about perception, and about painting.

DR: How is what you are drawing unique?
MG: This group of work is unique, I think, in its paradoxical way of dealing with the subject of war: It describes something almost beautiful that draws viewers in before they really understand what they are looking at.

DR: Do you set up constraints or rules to follow? If so, do you stick to your rules or break them? Why or why not?
MG: I do have rules for myself that I follow pretty strictly. I like working within constraints, whether self-imposed or intrinsic to the materials I work with.

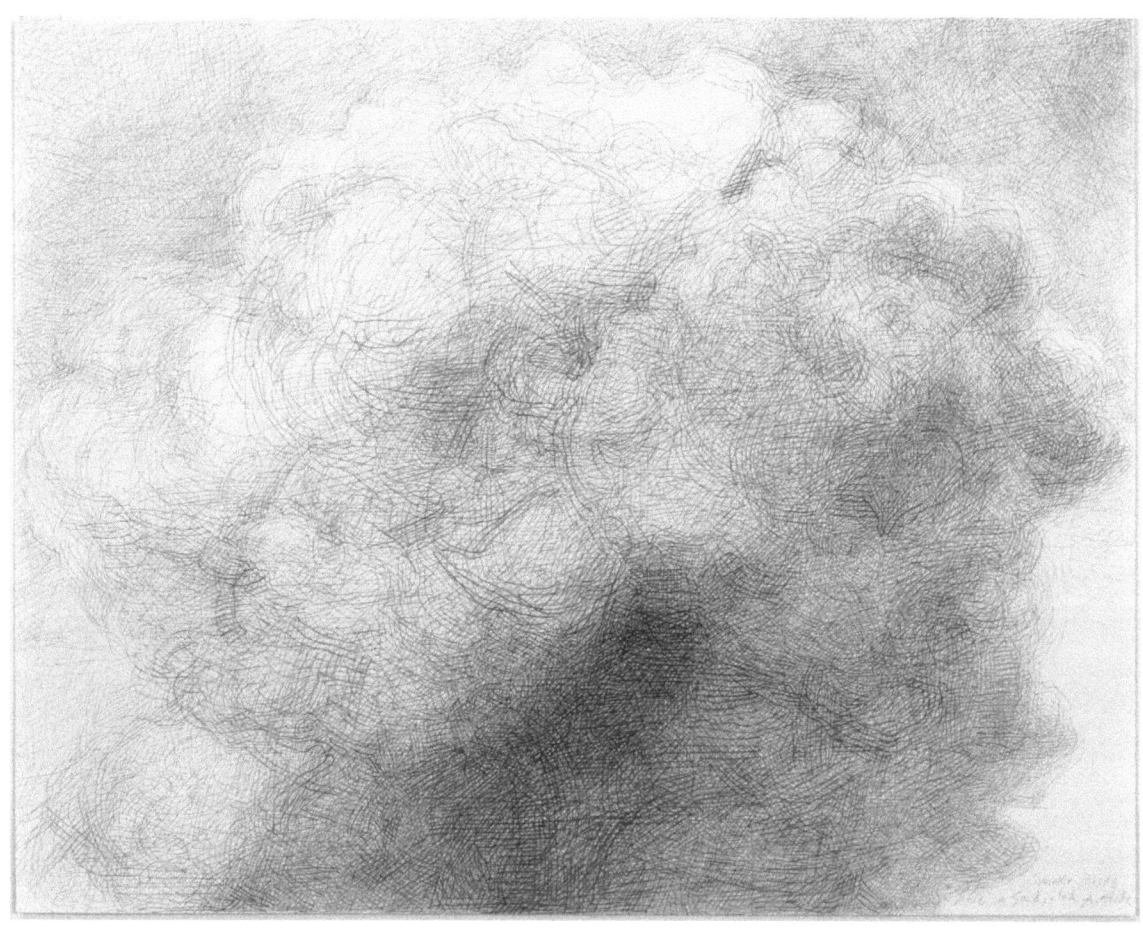

Smoke Rises From What Activists Say Was a Missile; 2015; Graphite; 11" x 14"

PAT BRENTANO

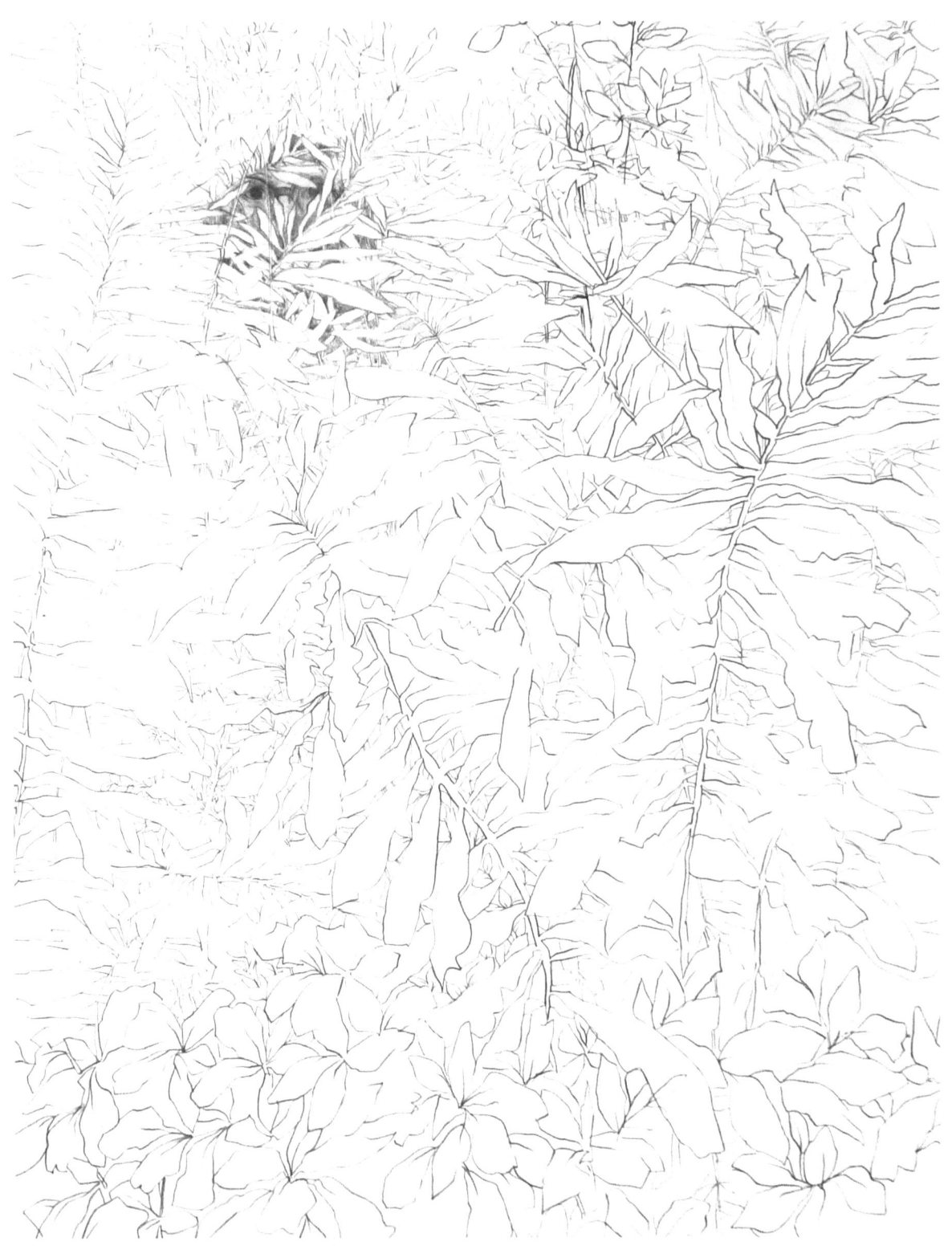

Hidden; 2015; Graphite; 37" x 50"

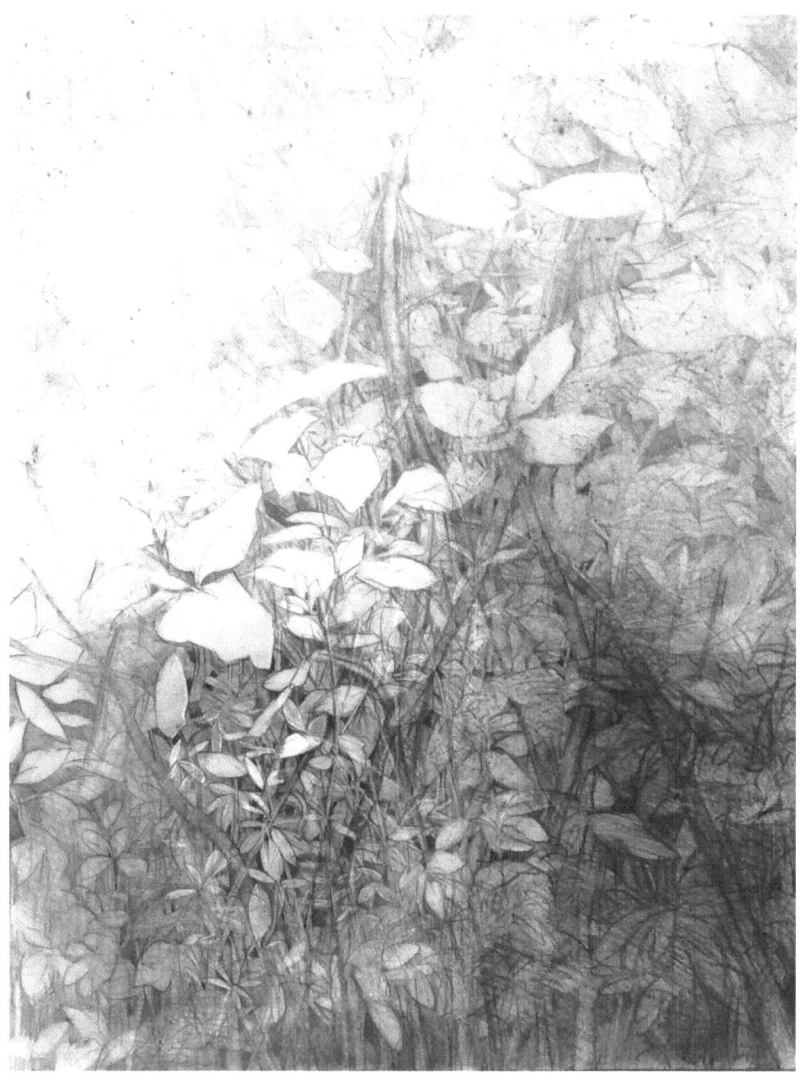

ABOUT

Obscured; 2015; Graphite; 37" x 50"

Raised and educated in southern Indiana, Pat developed a permanent connection to the natural world. Expressing this connection has been central to her work as an artist and educator. She was an assistant professor in drawing and painting at the University of Wisconsin, and an Adjunct Professor in drawing and painting at the University of Evansville and Kean University. Her drawings have been exhibited widely in museums and in curated exhibitions and galleries. In 2012 NJN State of the Arts produced a documentary about Pat as an artist and environmentalist, which aired nationally on PBS. The institute for Women's Leadership at Rutgers also produced a documentary about Pat's work as part of their Transforming Lives Project. She has collaborated with NJ Audubon and The Nature Conservancy to educate and inspire environmental responsibility through the visual arts and has received a number of grants awards and residencies and been a guest lecturer.

"The mystical rite of drawing has been my most personal and private mode of speech and primary activity since childhood. I am never without a sketchbook. It is the discipline that opens my inner eye and reveals the hidden realities of nature. The act of drawing strengthens my memory, inspires creative thought, and is the means by which I communicate my most visceral, personal vision. I want my artwork to speak for the birds, bees and pollinators that have lost their habitat due to our reckless behavior. The expressive act of drawing has the power to viscerally connect the viewer to nature, and reawaken their sensibilities. If I can make the audience see and feel the content of my artwork then they might reconsider their own personal connection to nature. I want to start the conversation about being part of something larger than us." - P. B.

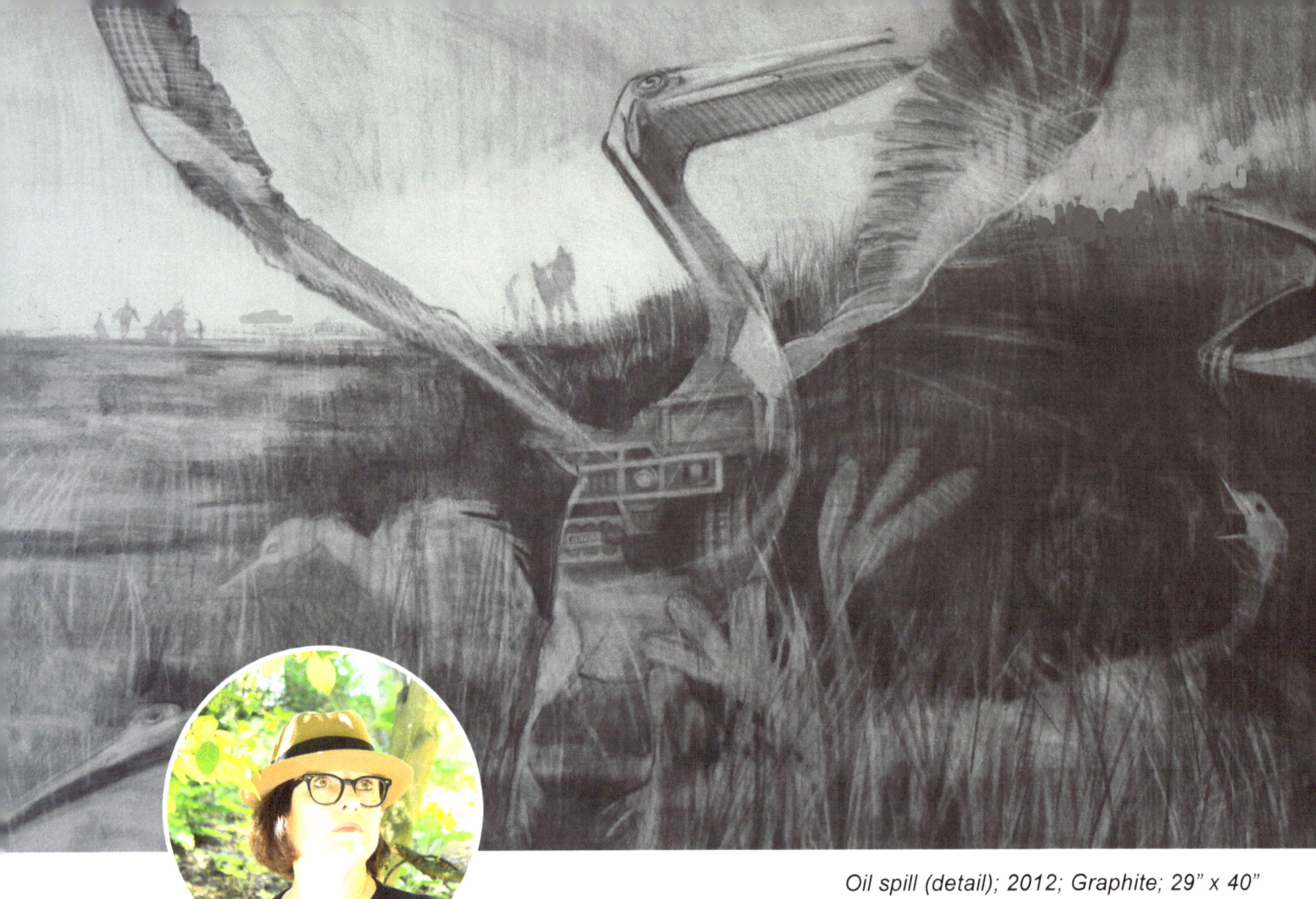

Oil spill (detail); 2012; Graphite; 29" x 40"

DRAWING ROOMS INTERVIEW

DR: What got you interested in drawing?
PB: Since I was a kid growing up in southern Indiana I have been interested in expressing my connection to the natural world. Drawing was my means of communicating those visual experiences.

DR: What is your intention in making these drawings?
PB: My intention is to speak for nature. I hope to educate and inspire responsible stewardship by visually re-connecting the viewer to the natural world through the visual language.

DR: Where does your exploration with drawing take you?
PB: My exploration with drawing takes me to the essence of the natural world through the heart of the visual language. It opens my inner eye and I am able to express the hidden realities of my most visceral observations.

DR: How is what you are drawing unique?
PB: My work is unique because it is created from direct observation using academic skills and techniques to express my most personal visual ideas.

DR: Do you set up constraints or rules to follow? If so, do you stick to your rules or break them? Why or why not?
PB: My rules are that I use my skill as an artist to elevate my message to the highest level possible and if I need to break those rules so be it.

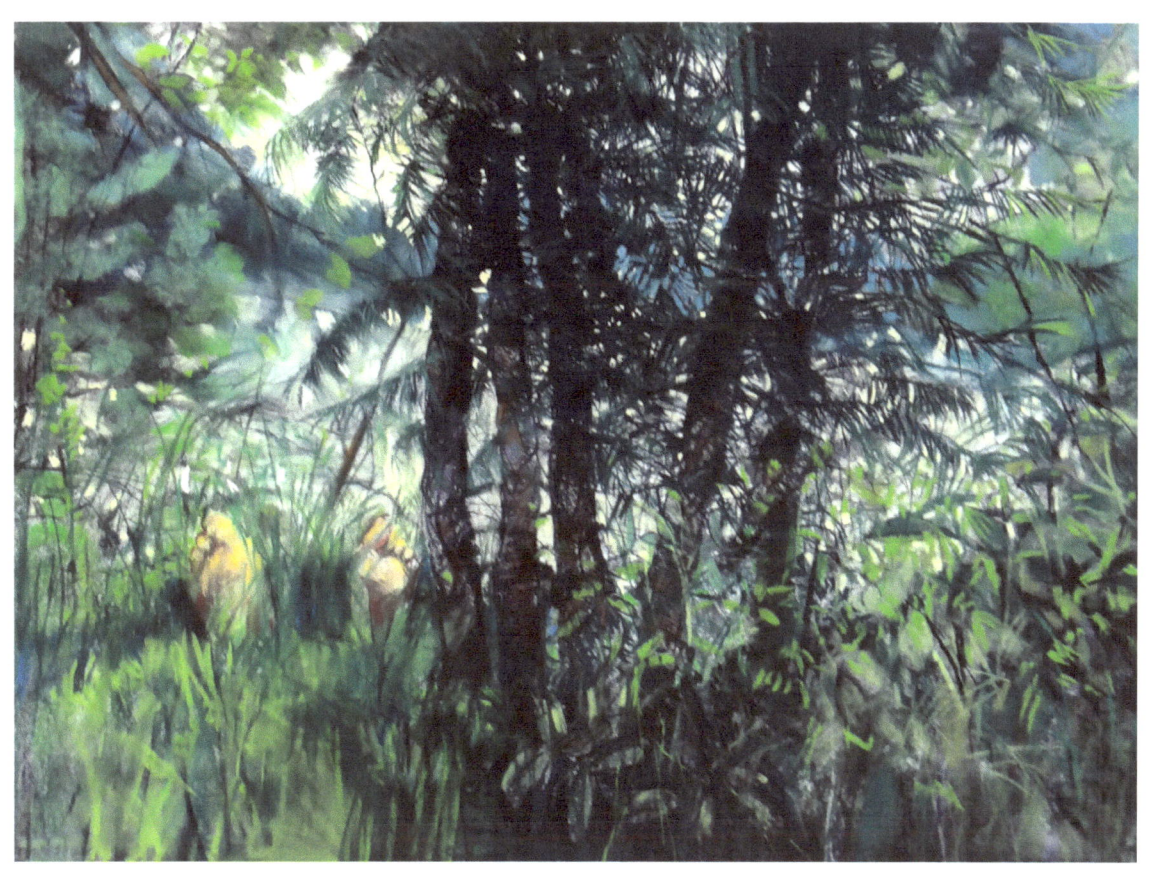

We are part of Nature; 2015; Charcoal and pastel; 37" x 50".

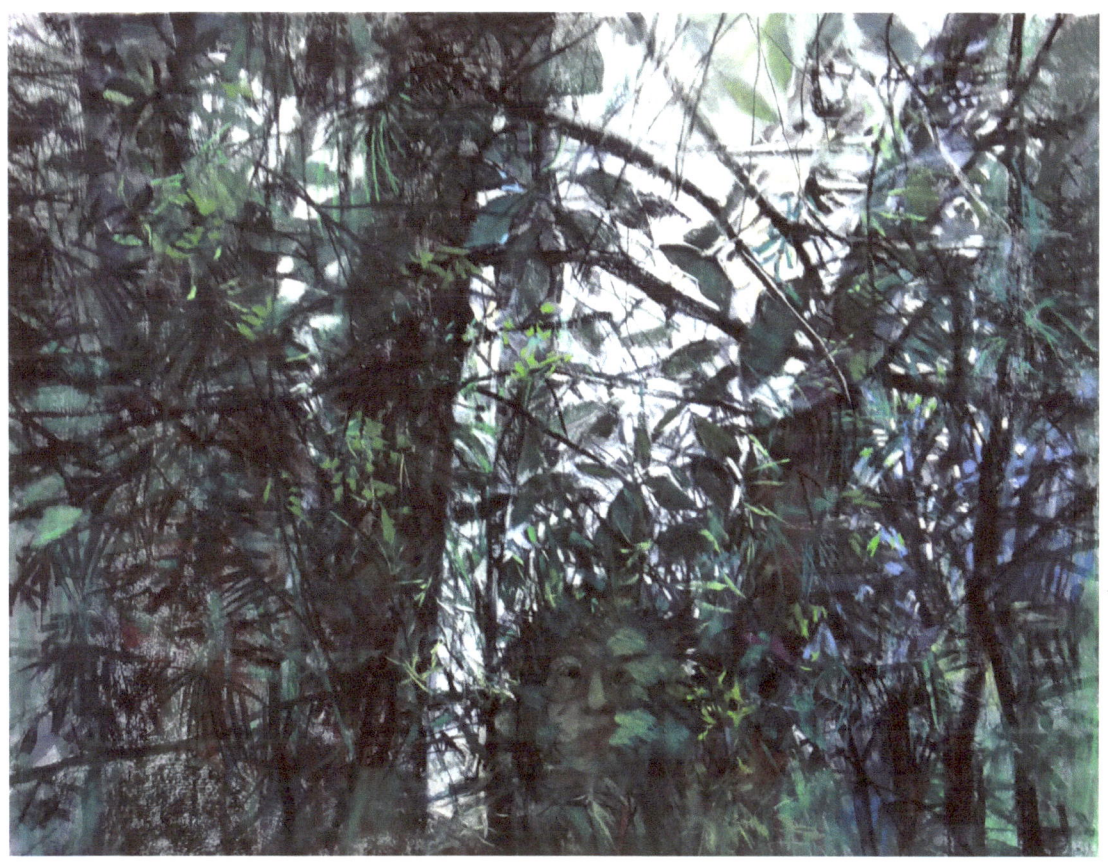

Are you aware of where you are?; 2015; Charcoal and pastel; 37" x 50"

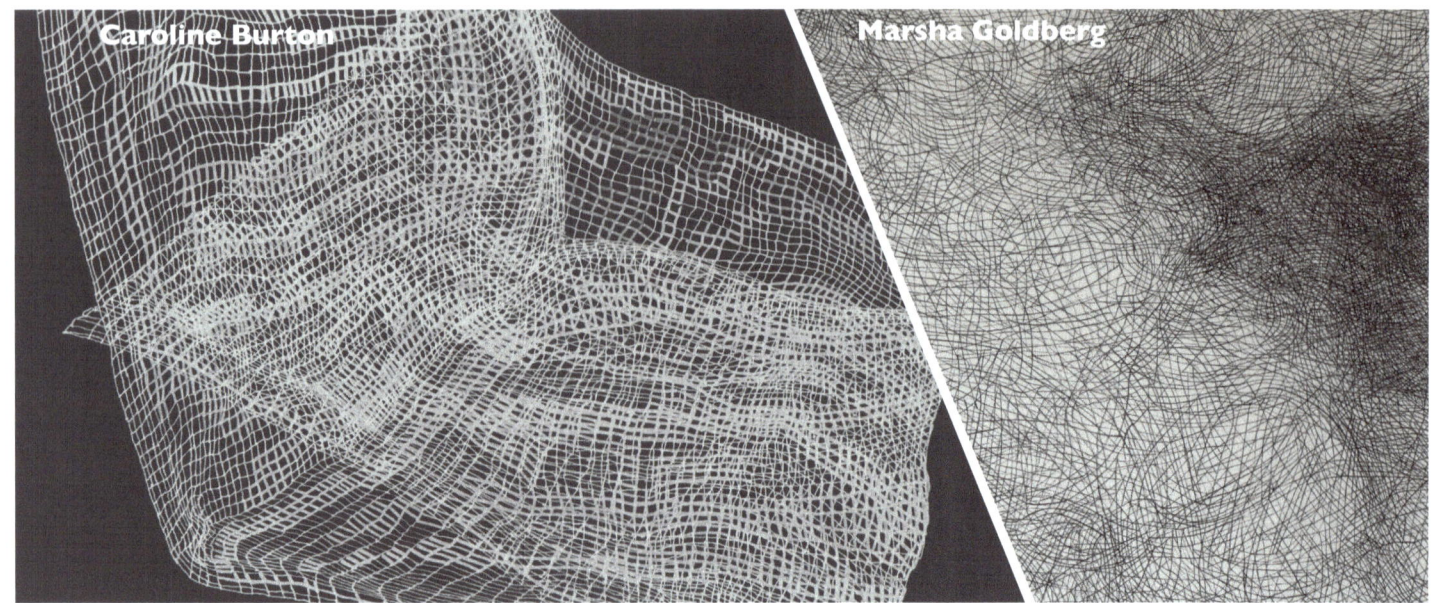

Caroline Burton

Marsha Goldberg

A STATEWIDE SURVEY OF

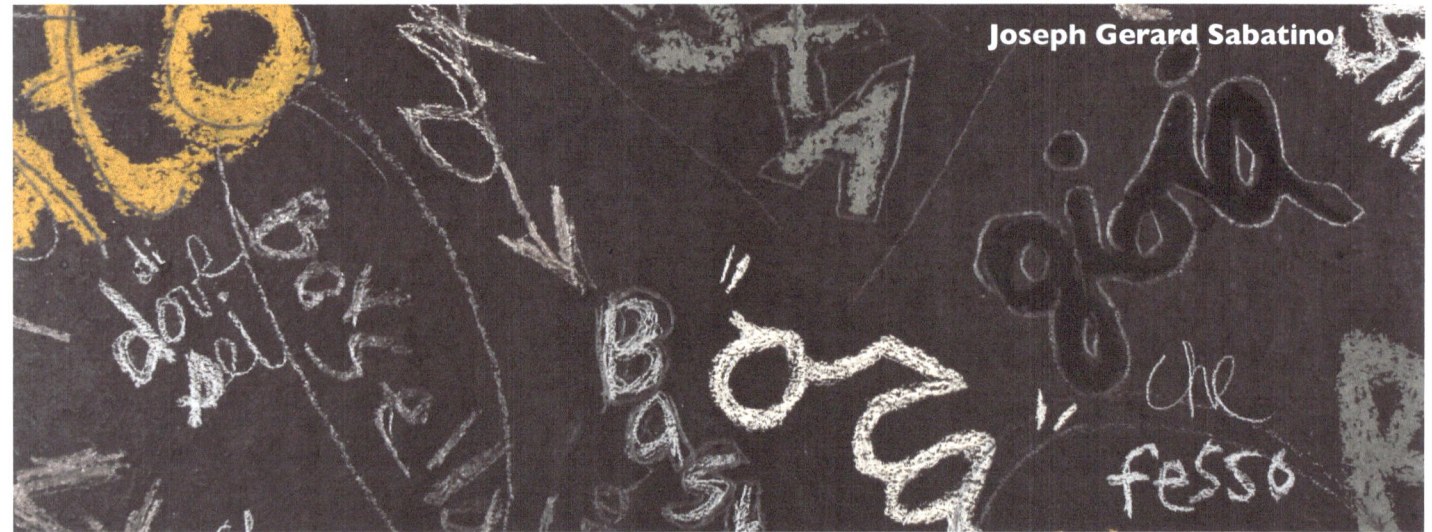

Joseph Gerard Sabatino

CONTEMPORARY DRAWING

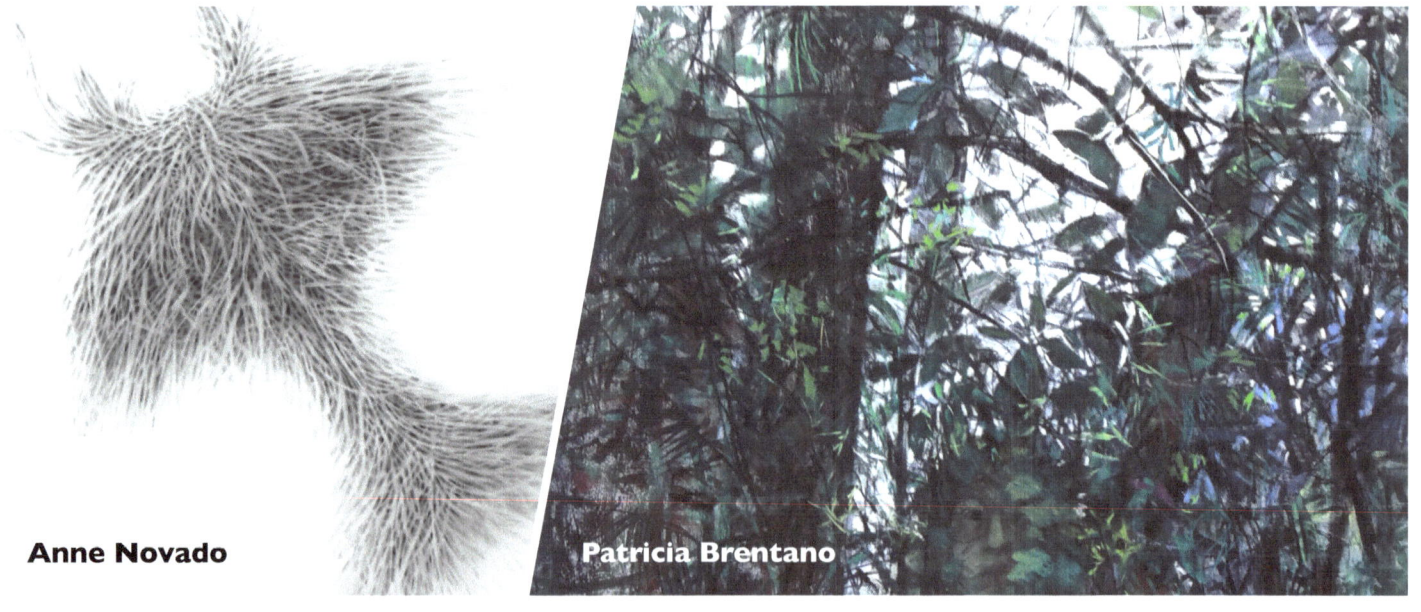

Anne Novado

Patricia Brentano

DRAWING ROOMS
DRAW-A-THON

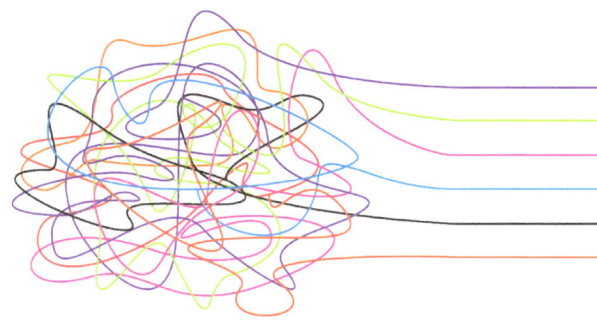

DRAWING THE COMMUNITY TOGETHER

DRAWING-TOGETHER PUBLIC PROJECTS

Victory Hall Inc. has created public art projects with professional area artists and students since 2008.

Our DRAW-A-THON events gather the community for a day of free art activities.

In our DRAWING-TOGETHER projects, area artists collaborate with school groups to design and create public drawing projects sponsored by businesses and displayed in public lobbies and work-spaces.

To find out about sponsoring a project, contact us at info@drawingrooms.org

VICTORY HALL INC. DRAWING ROOMS

180 Grand St.
Jersey City, NJ 07302

www.drawingrooms.org
victoryhall1@msn.com
201 823-9393

OPEN YEAR-ROUND:
Thursday & Friday 4pm to 7pm
Saturday & Sunday 2pm to 6pm

THANKS TO OUR SPONSORS AND SUPPORTERS 2015-16

The Geraldine R. Dodge Foundation
Qualcomm
Structuretone
City of Bayonne, CDBG
Hudson County LAP
Kay Cook and Perry Pogany
Mario and Anna Scipione
Patricia Rubino
Kenneth M Jacobs
Margaret Weber
Carol Pustorino
OLC Catholic Church

GOOD LUCK

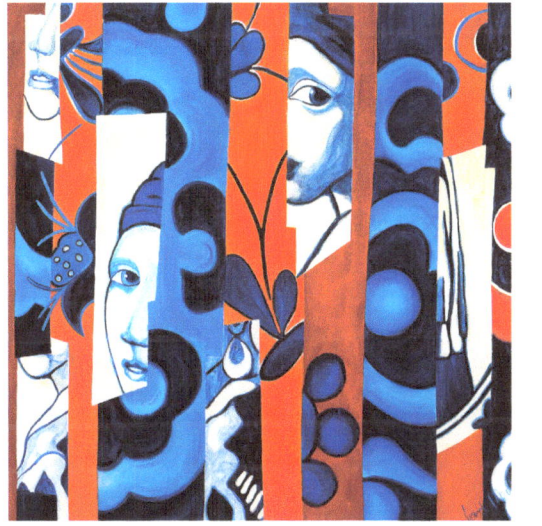

DRAWING ROOMS

Joe Cosenza and Loura van der Meule

louravandermeule.com

Loura van der Meule will be exhibiting her work in the Netherlands through the month of July 2016!

FIELDS
CONSTRUCTION COMPANY

SILVERMAN
BUILDING NEIGHBORHOODS

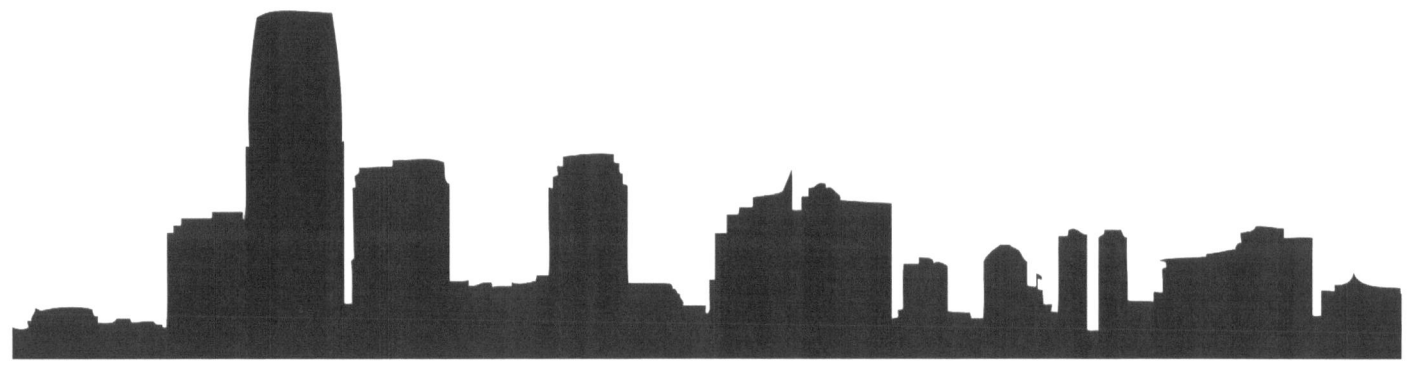

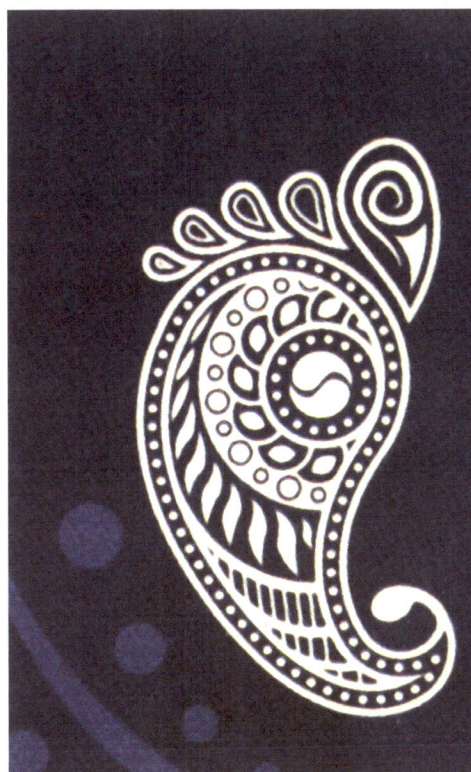
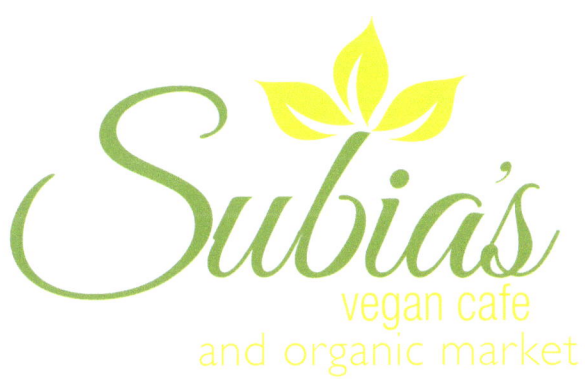
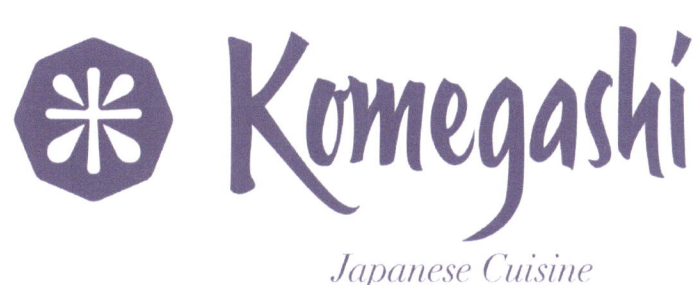

VICTORY HALL PRESS
180 Grand St.
Jersey City, NJ 07302
drawingrooms.org

Copyright © Victory Hall Press, May 2016
ISBN-13: 978-0692724774
ISBN-10: 069272477X

This program is made possible in part by funds from the New Jersey State Council on the Arts/ Department of State, a partner agency of the National Endowment for the Arts, administered by the Hudson County Office of Cultural and Heritage. Affairs, Thomas A. DeGise, County Executive, and the Board of Chosen Freeholders.